The
Trailer
Manual

The
Trailer
Manual

Brian Bate IEng MSOE MIRTE

**The complete guide to buying, maintaining
and building light trailers**

Author: Brian Bate
Project Manager: Louise McIntyre
Copy editor: Peter Nicholson
Page build: James Robertson

First published 2006

Published by: Haynes Publishing, Sparkford,
Yeovil, Somerset BA22 7JJ, UK

A catalogue record for this book is available
from the British Library

ISBN 1 84425 212 4

Printed in Great Britain by J. H. Haynes & Co. Ltd.

**While every effort is taken to ensure the
accuracy of the information given in this
book, no liability can be accepted by the
author or publishers for any loss, damage or
injury caused by errors in, or omissions
from, the information given.**

CONTENTS

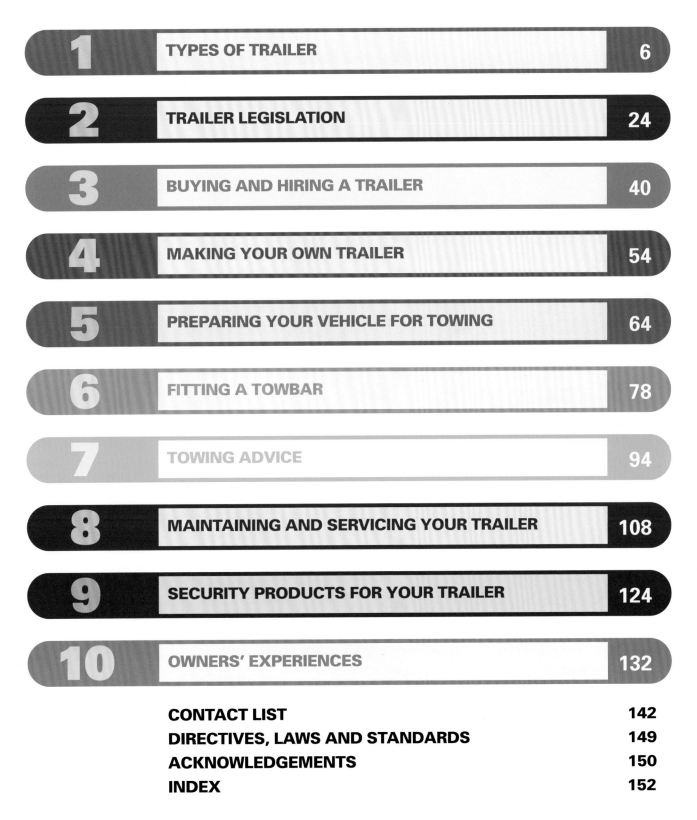

TYPES OF TRAILER

A trailer is probably the most versatile type of vehicle that has ever been built. It is also the oldest road vehicle of all with a direct lineage from the invention of the wheel.

1

Trailers can be designed to do any particular task in the most efficient way possible and we cover many different designs here. However, it is impossible to feature them all in this book, so only the main types from 250kg (550lb) to 3,500kg (7,717lb) are included.

Unbraked trailers

The first broad category of trailers are those under 750kg (1,654lb), which do not require brakes to be fitted. Several types are embraced under this heading and include the following examples.

GENERAL PURPOSE

The most commonly seen trailers are small general purpose types mainly used by house owners to carry garden refuse to a waste disposal depot or to fetch building materials from a merchant for a serious DIY project. This market is dominated by the lightweight all-metal designs from France, which are available in flat pack or fully assembled forms.

These can be fitted with extras such as a moulded plastic top or ladder racks.

One very useful extra is to have a drop-down tailboard, because it makes it so much easier to load and off-load materials from the trailer.

These products are also available with a manual tipping design, which adds further versatility.

You can, however, still buy a traditional British trailer that is made with a heavy-duty plywood floor and either ply or solid timber sides with a metal frame. These seem to last for ever and you can regularly see very old ones still in use.

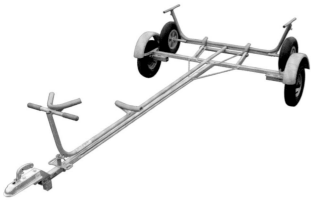

DINGHY/CANOE TRAILERS

They are really skeletal trailers, as they do not have any bodywork at all. For example, a dinghy trailer is built for the sole purpose of carrying a light boat and is available in differing lengths to suit the size and weight of dinghy that needs to be carried.

A similar trailer can have a frame built to carry canoes or rowing boats. These often have a locker added to carry oars, paddles, buoyancy aids and protective clothing.

TRAILER TENTS

These are remarkable trailers. They are so light yet unfold to offer a surprising amount of room for camping, and can even be towed by relatively small cars. Note the difference in size between a folded trailer tent and the same trailer when set up on a camping site. Yes, there is a trailer under there. Stuck for storage space? There are some models, which can be stored on their side.

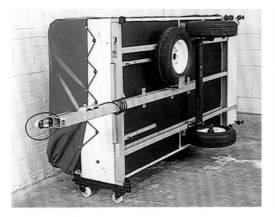

ALL-TERRAIN VEHICLE (ATV) TRAILERS
These are designed to carry ATV vehicles such as quad bikes. These are small, four-wheel motorcycles and were mainly used by farmers but many owners now use them for leisure activities.

MOBILITY TRAILERS
These trailers are designed to carry the electric scooters for disabled people thereby leaving room in the towing car for luggage and other passengers. The EZ Rise trailer has the advantage of having air suspension that can be lowered so that the scooter can be driven on easily. The suspension is then lifted using a 12V-air compressor. This trailer is fitted with castors enabling it to be taken through a doorway and stored on end. It represents a very neat solution for the elderly or infirm who need to use a trailer.

Another design of trailer that can be stored in a very small space is the Duuo Easy-Store. This is a small GP trailer where the body is lifted off the platform chassis and then the chassis is rolled into the body. The trailer is then lifted onto its castors and wheeled away for storage.

Braked trailers over 750kg (1,654lb)

While unbraked trailers have strict limitations of use due to weight restrictions, trailers fitted with a braking system offer considerably more scope for transporting heavier items. Many variants fall within this category including the following types.

GENERAL PURPOSE
These are the workhorses of the small business world and are used by builders, farmers and plant hire companies to carry anything and everything.

They are supplied in flatbed form, with drop sides or tipping (from the front or the side) with gross weights up to 3,500kg.

The heaviest are normally on twin axles but if there is a need to have a lower floor height three axles are used, which can be fitted with smaller wheels and tyres.

The only problem with a tri-axle trailer is that the wide spread (the distance between the front and rear wheel centres) can create excessive tyre scrub (sideways force on the tyre) when

manoeuvring. One interesting design that reduces the spread and scrub is to fit the central axle in between the first and third axles with a narrower track. This enables the wheels to overlap, so that the axles are all closer together thereby making the trailer much more manoeuvrable. This design is called the Centipede.

General purpose trailers can be supplied with a beaver tail (a downward sloping rear floor section) or a rear ramp.

Towing a small car behind a Motorhome

Some people with a motorhome use an 'A'-frame or a towing dolly to tow a small car on its wheels. It is illegal to transport a car in this way. (See Chapter 2 'A'-frames and dollies.)

The legal way to tow behind a motorhome is to use a basic car transporter.

CAR TRANSPORTERS

This type of trailer is the most popular one hired from trailer centres and it is made in a range of sizes. Some will carry a very small car; others can carry large vehicles.

You can have a car transporter with lift-up ramps or with slide-out ramps or have fully enclosing bodywork. They can also be made with a hydraulic tilt bed for easier loading and unloading. If you have a need to carry lightweight cars you can even get one that carries two!

GLIDER TRAILERS
The longest trailers allowed (see Chapter 2) under 3,500 kg are those built to carry gliders.

HORSE TRAILERS

This is another extremely popular design. These trailers are made to carry one, two and even three horses, the Ifor Williams Hunter range, for example, being particularly popular.

In addition to standard versions you can have bespoke designs of horse trailers made to suit your exact needs. People who take part in carriage driving competitions in particular purchase these, because the carriage has to be transported in the trailer as well as the horse.

The largest of these designs can also incorporate living accommodation, where either the front or rear part of the trailer converts to living space after the carriage has been taken out. This is a very useful design for the regular competitor since it eliminates the need and cost of hotel accommodation.

BOAT TRAILERS

These are made in skeletal form and are available in a wide range of sizes to suit all types of boat. They can either have a fixed bed or a breakback design where the trailer tilts to allow the boat to be lowered into the water so that it can be floated off.

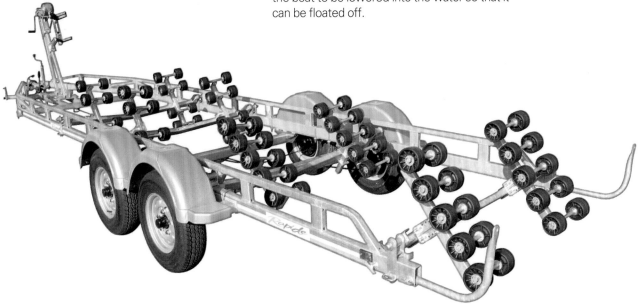

BOX VAN TRAILERS

This type of braked trailer is another workhorse for small businesses. It permits the user to significantly augment the carrying capacity of a normal Transit-type van without employing another driver and powered vehicle.

Box vans are popular hire vehicles for people who are moving house and help to reduce removal costs. They are available with the bodywork constructed either between or over the wheels.

LIVESTOCK TRAILERS

The Ifor Williams livestock trailer is commonly seen in rural locations throughout this country. In market towns on market day you would think that a rally was being held for them, as there will be so many of them there. These trailers come in a range of sizes from small ones catering for sheep or pigs to large, tri-axle ones for cattle.

CATERING TRAILERS

This type of trailer demonstrates the extreme diversity of design from small units to the very largest with extremely elaborate bodywork. An offshoot of this type of trailer is the market stall. These embody a very clever design that allows a small trailer to convert into a large covered stall.

EXHIBITION AND HOSPITALITY TRAILERS

These are very useful vehicles for the business world and again, incorporate some very clever ideas to gain space. Slide-out sides and fold-out flaps can create a huge area for maximum promotional purposes. This type of trailer is often used for mobile laboratories and police incident work.

MOTORCYCLE TRAILERS

There are two types of trailer classed as motorcycle trailers: those that carry motorcycles and those towed behind a motorcycle. The former can be supplied to carry one, two or three motorcycles.

A solo motorcycle with an engine capacity above 125cc is allowed to tow a trailer although these are restricted in size and weight. A motorcycle sidecar outfit can tow a normal sized trailer within set weight limits.

ADVERTISING TRAILERS
These are seen more and more parked on the side of the road or in fields besides motorways doing their job of advertising.

PLANT TRAILERS
Building trade and construction companies often use trailers to carry specialised types of plant machinery. They are available with rear ramps or you can have one where the load bed lowers down to ground level for easy loading.

Another type is known as a mobile plant trailer where the trailer is simply a 'T'-frame chassis with the type of plant carried, such as an air compressor, mobile generator and a water bowser simply bolted to it. These trailers are not designed to carry any other items so may be exempt from the Tachograph regulations. (See Chapter 2.)

FOLDING CARAVAN/CAMPER TRAILERS
These are larger versions of the trailer tent detailed earlier. They are usually referred to as trailers although they are more similar to a caravan on account of the fact that the sides are made of an aluminium and foam sandwich rather than fabric.

Alternative axle layouts

Most trailers have the wheels positioned approximately under the centre point of the bodywork, but there are alternative arrangements. You can have a trailer with one or two axles at the back and another at the front. The front axle can then be on a turntable fixed to the drawbar so that the whole axle pivots about its centre.

On another design, the front wheels steer, using the Ackerman principle. In this type the drawbar is attached to a linkage, which operates steering arms attached to the front hubs as shown here.

The final design is the fifth wheel type, sometimes referred to as semi-trailers. These are really downsized articulated trailers pulled by pick-up trucks or chassis-cab light commercial vehicles. They give extra space and are very manoeuvrable.

As you can see from the above examples, trailers really *do* come in many types, shapes and sizes. You never know what they will carry but you can have surprises.

I have not covered all designs, but you can always have a bespoke design of trailer made to do exactly whatever you want it to do. That is the beauty of trailers; you can literally have anything you want. You cannot always do this with a powered vehicle, because the cost can be prohibitive.

TRAILER LEGISLATION

Any vehicle used on the road must conform to a variety of regulations. Trailers are no exception, especially as they are legally defined under European Regulations as vehicles in their own right.

The legislation may seem onerous, but the intention is to provide trailers that are built to do a job safely.

Trailers, used in the United Kingdom and towed by UK-registered vehicles must meet requirements laid down in the *Road Vehicles (Construction and Use) Regulations 1986 (SI 1986 No. 1078)* and amending regulations as well as the *Road Vehicles Lighting Regulations 1989 (SI 1989 No. 1796)* as amended.

Although there are some 'grey' areas in the current legislation, this chapter highlights some of the more important aspects.

Weights

MAXIMUM WEIGHTS

Unbraked trailers (Type 01) can be used up to a maximum weight of 750kg (1,654lb).

Note: A vehicle can only tow an unbraked trailer loaded to half the towing vehicle's kerb weight. To tow a 750kg gross vehicle weight (GVW) trailer a vehicle must have a kerb weight of at least 1,500kg (3,300lb). If your car weighs 1,000kg (2,200lb) you are restricted to a loaded trailer weight of 500kg (1,100lb).

A solo motorcycle, with an engine capacity exceeding 125cc, can tow an unbraked trailer up to a maximum weight of 150kg (330lb) *or* two thirds of the kerb weight of the motorcycle, *whichever is the less*. The kerb weight must be clearly marked on the nearside of the motorcycle.

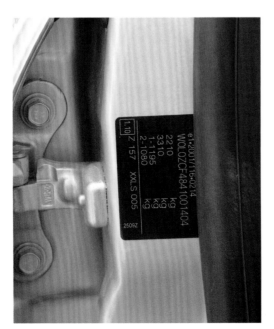

A typical car VIN plate.

Braked trailers (Type 02) can be used up to a maximum of 3,500kg (7,700lb).

Your vehicle's unbraked and braked towing limits will be found in the handbook or on its vehicle identification number (VIN) plate.

NOSE WEIGHT

Your vehicle manufacturer will state the figures for maximum nose weight in the handbook.

If for any reason, you don't have access to your vehicle's owner's handbook to check the figures for your vehicle, have a look at the VIN plate, usually found under the bonnet or on a door pillar.

Alternatively, if you are thinking of changing your car and cannot find this information from a car dealer, ring up the manufacturer's technical department for the information. Do not rely on manufacturer's brochures, as they will often give a maximum towing limit without indicating if there are any conditions regarding passengers or luggage

The given towing limit is usually *with just a driver on board* weighing 68kg (150lb) plus 7kg (15lb) of luggage on board *(European Directive 95/48/EC)*. Any change from this situation, either by carrying extra passengers or luggage *will reduce this limit by their individual weights*. Always have a look at a car's handbook and read the 'towing' section before deciding which car to buy. Note that Vauxhall are currently giving towing limits with two people on-board weighing 70kg each.

If you exceed any of the above maximum limits you are breaking the law by having an overloaded vehicle. In addition, your insurance company can invalidate your insurance if it was found, following an accident, that you had an overloaded vehicle. It could be a very expensive mistake, so ensure that you operate within the nose weight and towing limits of your vehicle at all times.

Dimensions

When towing with a vehicle having a GVW of up to 3,500kg a trailer may have a maximum length of 7m (23ft) excluding the drawbar and a maximum width of 2.3m (7ft 6in) unless being towed by a vehicle with a GVW exceeding 3,500kg, when an overall trailer width of 2.55m (8ft 4in) and length of 12m (39ft 4in), excluding the drawbar, is allowed.

Note: In law, only metric measurements can

be used; imperial measurements are shown here purely as a comparison.

You can exceed the 7m length limit if your trailer has been specially built to carry an indivisible load i.e. a load that cannot be split into smaller sections, such as a glider trailer, where the glider's fuselage is longer than 7m. The trailer can only be used for this purpose.

A trailer towed by a solo motorcycle has a different length restriction. In this case the distance between the rearmost part of the trailer and the motorcycle's rear wheel spindle must not exceed 2.5m. The overall width of the trailer must not exceed 1m.

Overhang and wide loads

These terms usually apply to large boats with a wide beam but long lengths of timber, roof trusses or ladders can bring you into this part of the Regulations. Loads may overhang the sides

of a trailer by no more than 305mm (1ft), but the overall width of the trailer and load must not exceed 2.9m (9ft 6in).

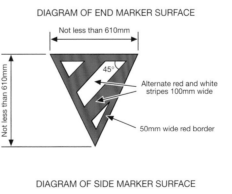

DIAGRAM OF END MARKER SURFACE

Not less than 610mm

Not less than 610mm

45°

Alternate red and white stripes 100mm wide

50mm wide red border

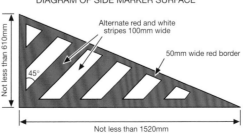

DIAGRAM OF SIDE MARKER SURFACE

Not less than 610mm

Alternate red and white stripes 100mm wide

50mm wide red border

45°

Not less than 1520mm

A Squire trailer built to the maximum 1m width.

If you have a load to carry that is wider than this, an exception is made to allow you to go up to 4.3m (14ft) if two clear working days notice prior to the date the journey is to begin, is given to the chief officer of police for any area in which you propose to use the vehicle. In such cases, marker boards should be fitted within 50mm (2in) of the edge of the load at the front and rear *(Regulation 81 and 82 Schedule 12)*, which must be clearly visible.

If the load is wider than 3.5m (11ft 6in) then an attendant must be carried. They need to be there to get out of the cab to instruct the driver verbally or by using hand signals if the vehicle has to negotiate narrow roads, travel past obstructions or under low bridges etc.

When travelling at night the marker boards must be illuminated, but the light of the lamps themselves must not be visible to other road users *(Regulations 81* and *82 Schedule 12)*. Loads may project forwards by up to 2m (6ft 6in) before any need for marker boards. These are required if the projection exceeds 2m but not exceeding 3.05m (10ft) and an attendant must be carried.

Rearward projecting loads may go up to 1m without any need to warn other road users. If the projection exceeds this length but is not more than 2m in excess then steps must be

taken to make the projection clearly visible although there is no legislation saying what you need to do. Usually, a piece of brightly coloured cloth is sufficient to do this.

If the projection exceeds 2m but does not exceed 3.05m, end marker boards must be fitted. If the projection exceeds 3.05m, end and side markers must be fitted, an attendant carried and the two working days notice given to the Police, as described above.

There is no limit to the height of a trailer or a trailer plus its load. If, however, the height exceeds 3m then the towing vehicle must have either (a) a notice displayed in a prominent position in the driving cab showing the overall travelling height of the vehicle, its load or equipment, or (b) documents in the cab, within easy reach of the driver, giving details of the route, or choice of routes, to be taken so as to eliminate the risk of the vehicle, its load or equipment, from striking bridges or other overhead structures during the course of the journey.

If (a) is adopted the notice must show the overall travelling height in feet and inches, or in both feet and inches and metres; the numbers used for giving the height in feet and inches must be at least 40mm (1$\frac{3}{4}$in) tall and those used for giving the height in both feet and inches and metres must not differ by more than 50mm *(Regulation 10)*.

Brakes

Type 02 trailers must be fitted with a braking system, which complies with European Community *Braking Directive 71/320/EC* and amendments *75/524/EC and 79/489/EC*. These directives lay down technical standards on braking and stopping stability, and downhill speed control. Trailers manufactured from 1 October 1988 must be fitted with automatic reversing brakes.

The parking brake must apply to at least two wheels and be capable of holding a stationary trailer on a gradient of at least one in 6.25 without the assistance of stored energy. Stored energy is any residual force being applied by spring or hydraulic means. The stored energy in the overrun brake linkage is not included here, as the residual force will have been used up when applying the extra brake rod movement needed if the handbrake has been applied immediately after reversing a trailer. A person standing on the ground must be able to operate the brakes by a means of operation (handbrake lever) fitted to the trailer *(Regulation 16 and Schedule 3)*. European Directive 98/12/EC now

Steel cable secondary coupling.

requires all friction material used on trailer brakes to be asbestos free.

A trailer, when detached from its towing vehicle, must be prevented from moving either by the use of a handbrake, chain, chock or other efficient device being applied to at least one of its wheels *(Regulation 89)*. This applies to unbraked trailers as well.

Secondary couplings

A secondary coupling is either a chain or cable on unbraked trailers or a breakaway cable on braked trailers.

Braked trailers manufactured from 1 October 1982 can only be used on the road if they are fitted with a device, which stops them automatically if the main coupling between the towing vehicle and trailer breaks and the vehicles separate, i.e. a breakaway cable. A breakaway cable applies the brakes fully, if the trailer becomes detached from the towing vehicle, and the cable then breaks allowing the trailer to separate itself from the towing vehicle.

Unbraked trailers manufactured from 1 January 1997 having a GVW not exceeding 750kg must have a secondary coupling fitted which, if the main coupling breaks, prevents the drawbar from touching the ground and some steering remains on the trailer. In other words, it keeps the trailer attached to the vehicle.

Plates

Every unbraked trailer must have a maker's plate attached marked with its maximum gross weight in kilograms displayed in a conspicuous and readily accessible position on the left or nearside. The MGW refers to the weight which it is designed or adapted not to exceed when used on the road laden *(Regulation 71)*.

Unbraked trailers made from 1 January 1997 with a GVW up to 750kg must also be marked with the year of manufacture on the nearside in such a way that the marking cannot be obliterated *(Regulation 71A)*.

Here's a typical unbraked trailer plate. It shows the serial number, gross weight of 400kg, nose weight of 75kg and made in 1998.

The Department for Transport requires manufacturer's plates to be fitted to braked trailers for safety recall purposes. These plates must show:

- Manufacturer's name
- Chassis or serial number
- Number of axles
- Maximum weight for each axle
- Maximum load imposed on drawing vehicle (Nose weight)
- Maximum gross weight (GVW)
- Year of manufacture

Manufacturers usually add on the tyre size and pressure as well.

Note: If a plate is not attached the Police will use the maximum weight shown on the coupling to determine the gross vehicle weight. This may be higher than the trailer's capacity as couplings are made for weight bands and may cause you problems with tachograph or driving licence regulations.

Tyres

The tyres are one of the most important components of a trailer – yet often, the most neglected.

Trailer tyres, with specialised exceptions, must be pneumatic. No trailer may be used on the road when fitted with pneumatic tyres if:

- The tyre is unsuitable for the use to which the trailer is being put or the type of tyre does not match tyres fitted to the other wheels.
- It is not properly inflated.
- The tyre has a cut of more than 25mm or 10% of its section width, whichever is greater, measured in any direction on the outside of the tyre and deep enough to reach the ply or cord.
- It has any lump, bulge or tear caused by separation or partial structural failure.
- The ply or cord is exposed.
- The grooves in the tread pattern must not go below a minimum of 1.6mm in depth throughout a continuous band situated in the central three quarters of the breadth of tread and round the entire outer circumference of the tyre.

Trailers must be fitted with tyres designed to support adequately the maximum axle weight when towed at the maximum speeds allowed for trailers. The tyres used on trailers are not, in many cases, of the same construction as car tyres of similar size. The two wheels on a single axle trailer might have to support the same weight as the four wheels on the tow car. It is illegal to use tyres that are not 'E' marked to show that they comply with the load and speed requirements of *ECE Regulation 30*. Re-treaded tyres, if used, have to be made to *British Standard BS AU144e: 1988,* and bear this mark.

The sale and supply of used tyres whether re-treaded or not are regulated and it is an offence for such tyres to be fitted to trailers unless certain conditions are satisfied. Exemptions from the regulations apply in certain circumstances *(The Motor Vehicles Tyres (Safety) Regulations 1994) (SI 1994 No. 3117).*

Mudguards

All trailers must be fitted with mudguards unless the bodywork affords suitable protection.

No mudguards needed here as the body extends over the wheels.

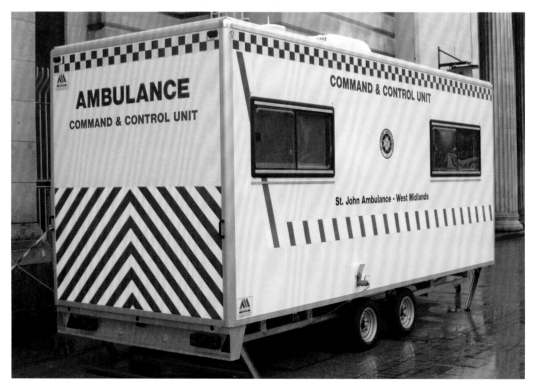

Maintenance, use of vehicle and security of load

Every trailer, together with all parts and accessories and the load carried, must at all times, be in such a condition that no danger or nuisance is caused, or is likely to be caused, to any person on the trailer or the road. Loads must be made secure; that is, loose loads sheeted and all loads physically restrained other than by their own weight, if necessary, to ensure against any part of the load falling or being blown from the vehicle *(Regulation 100)*.

A trailer may not be used for carrying passengers *(Regulation 90)*.

Type approval

Unlike cars, there is no compulsory type-approval scheme in the UK for trailers. The *Road Vehicles (Construction and Use Regulations) 1986 (SI 1986 No. 1078)* in the UK is aligned with EC directives so that they are identical in all material respects.

It is planned that there will be mandatory type approvals coming in to force for light trailers around 2010 to 2012. Imported trailers from European Community (EC) manufacturers will comply with UK regulations if they are made to EC type approvals, EC directives or their own country's equivalent. It is this non-compulsory Type Approval situation that allows the import of American trailers that do not meet EC directives or our own construction and use regulations even though they are not legal for use on our roads.

Lighting requirements

Legislation affecting the lighting of trailers is contained in the *Road Traffic Act 1988 s.41*, and the *Road Vehicles Lighting Regulations 1989 (SI 1989 No. 1796)* as amended.

OBLIGATORY LIGHTS
All trailers must have the following lighting and reflectors fitted:

■ Two front white reflectors (except for trailers under 1,600mm or for boat trailers and

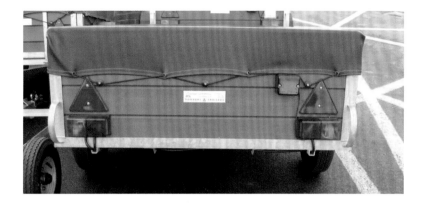

trailers less than 2,300mm long, made before October 1985).
■ Two front white position lights (except for trailers under 1,600mm or for boat trailers and trailers less than 2,300mm long, made before October 1985).
■ Two rear red triangular reflectors.
■ Two rear red sidelights.
■ Two rear red stoplights/brake lights.
■ Two rear amber direction indicator lamps.
■ One or two numberplate lights (if sufficient illumination is provided clear lens inserts can be used in the rear lamp clusters).
■ One or two rear red fog lights (except for trailers less than 1,300mm wide and trailers made before October 1985).
■ Two front and rear outline marker lights for trailers over 2,100mm wide manufactured since October 1991.

The reason that boat trailers do not have lights fitted is that people have the habit of reversing a loaded boat trailer into the water to unload the boat! Water and electricity do not go together so they have to use a rear trailer lighting board instead.

Info

Note: when purchasing a trailer lighting board do not buy a cycle lighting board by mistake (used on cars when cycles being carried on the back of a car obscure the lights). *A trailer lighting board must have triangular reflectors.* A cycle board must *not* have triangular ones. Be careful and ensure that you buy a board of the correct width, as the lamps must still comply with the position dimensions, for the lights, from the side of the trailer. (See below.)

ADDITIONAL LIGHTING REQUIREMENTS:

- Trailers longer than 6m (19ft 6in), excluding the drawbar, must have side marker lights *(except for boat trailers)*
- Trailers longer than 5m (16ft 3in). excluding the drawbar, must have amber side reflectors

The forward-most light or reflector must be no more than 4m (13ft) from the towball coupling with the rearmost one no more than 1m (3ft 3in) from the rear of the trailer. The distance separation must be no more than 3m (9ft 10in) between adjacent units. Fit additional ones if necessary.

All lighting must be kept clean and in working order at all times. The lights must be visible and working at all times at night and not be obscured by doors, when open, or by ramps when lowered. If any lights are obscured then duplicate lights may be fitted above the door or ramp as required.

All lights and reflectors on trailer manufactured from 1 October 1985 must be type approved and bear the 'e' mark followed by the number of the country that tested the lamps e.g. e11 is the UK mark.

POSITION OF LIGHTS

Front-position lights *(Schedule 2)*

Front-position (side) lights (white) must be fitted not more than 150mm from the side and not more than 1,500mm above the ground, or 2,100mm if the structure of the trailer precludes this. The horizontal angle of visibility must be 80° outwards and 5° inwards with a vertical angle of visibility 15° above and below the horizontal or 5° below if the lamp is less than 750mm from the ground.

The unique triangular reflector denotes a trailer.

Rear-position lights *(Schedule 10)*

Rear-position (tail) lights (red) must be fitted at or near the rear no more than 400mm from the side of the trailer with a minimum separation distance between the lamps of 500mm (400mm if the width is less than 1,400mm) and at a maximum height of 1,500mm (2,100mm if the structure of the trailer precludes this).

The horizontal angle of visibility must be 80° outwards and 45° inwards. The vertical angle of visibility 15° above and below the horizontal (or 10° below if less than 1,500mm from the ground or 5° below if less than 750mm from the ground).

Rear fog lamps *(Schedule 11)*

One or two rear red fog lamps must be fitted to trailers made from 1 October 1985 and if one is used it must be positioned from a central position to the offside of the trailer at or near the rear of the trailer. If two are fitted they shall form a matched pair. The maximum height from the ground is 1,000mm. There must be 100mm separation distance between the light emitting surfaces of the fog and stop lamps whether they are contained in a common body or are separate when viewed in a direction parallel to the longitudinal axis of the trailer. The horizontal angle of visibility is 25º inwards and outwards. The vertical angle of visibility is 5º above and below the horizontal.

It is illegal to have the fog light operated by the application of the braking system of the tow vehicle. Rear fog lamps may only be used when visibility is seriously reduced so as not to dazzle or inconvenience other road users. They must not be used when parked.

Stop lamps *(Schedule 12)*

At least two stop lamps (red) must be fitted to form a pair and must be positioned at least 400mm apart, one on each side of the longitudinal axis of the trailer and at a minimum height of 350mm and a maximum of 1,500mm (2,100mm if the structure of the trailer precludes this).

The horizontal angle of visibility is 45° to the left and right and 15° above and below the horizontal (or 10° if the lamp is less than 1,500mm from the ground or 5° if less than 750mm from the ground).

Stop lamps on both vehicles must operate when the brakes are applied.

Rear retro reflectors *(Schedule 18)*

Trailers must have two red reflectors positioned at or near the rear of the trailer; these must be vertical and face squarely to the rear. They may be positioned up to 400mm from the side of the trailer with a minimum separation distance between the pair of 600mm (or 400mm if the trailer is less than 1,400mm wide). The vertical position is a minimum of 350mm and a maximum of 900mm (or 2,100mm if the vehicle structure makes this impracticable).

The horizontal angle of visibility is 30° inwards and outwards and vertically 15° above and below the horizontal (or 5° below if the reflector is less than 750mm from the ground).

From 1 April 1991 rear reflectors must bear an approval mark incorporating 'III' or 'IIIA'

Front retro reflectors *(Schedule 21)*
All trailers manufactured from 1 October 1990 must be fitted with at least two white retro reflectors which are positioned up to 150mm from the side of the trailer with a minimum separation distance between the pair of 600mm (or 400mm if the trailer is less than 1,400mm). The minimum height from the ground is 350mm and the maximum is 900mm (or 1,500mm if the structure makes this impractical).

The horizontal angle of visibility is 30° outwards and 5° inwards and vertically 15° above and below the horizontal (or 5° below if the reflector is less than 750mm from the ground). Triangular reflectors must not be fitted to the front of any trailer.

Direction indicators *(Schedule 7)*
Trailers must have a pair of amber rear indicators marked on the lens with the figure '2', '2a' or '2b' above the approval mark. They must be positioned up to 400mm from the side of the trailer with a minimum separation distance between the pair of 500mm (or 400mm if the trailer is less than 1,400mm wide) and between 350mm and 1,500mm from the ground (up to 2,300mm if the structure of the trailer precludes this). The horizontal angle of visibility is 80° outwards and 45° inwards and vertically 15° above and below the horizontal.

Side repeater indicators can be fitted to trailers within 2,600mm of the front of the trailer and the lamps must have the figure '5' above the approval mark. The lights must flash at the same rate as the car's indicator lights. The driver of the vehicle must have a 'tell-tale' in the car showing that a trailer's indicator lamps are working correctly. This can take the form of a lamp or an audible buzzer. *(Schedule 7 Part 1, Clause 11)*

Rear registration plate lamp *(Schedule 15)*
Trailers must have a white lamp that adequately illuminates the numberplate, but it must be set so that it does not dazzle or cause discomfort to other road users.

Outline marker lights *(Schedule 13 Pt II)*
Outline marker lights must show white to the front and red to the rear. They can be combined into a lamp that shows white to the front and red to the rear. They must be mounted no more than 400mm from the side of the trailer. The horizontal angle of visibility is 80° outwards and 0° inwards. The vertical angle of visibility is 5° above and 20° below the horizontal.

Side marker lights *(Regulations 19, 22 and Schedule 9)*
Where fitted they must be mounted on each side, be amber in colour and positioned at a maximum distance from the front of the trailer of 4m including the drawbar. The maximum distance from the rear of the trailer of the rearmost side marker lamp is 1m. The maximum separation distance between the light-emitting surfaces of adjacent side marker lamps on the same side of the trailer is 3m or, if this is not practical, 4m. They must be mounted no more than 2,300mm from the ground. The horizontal angle of visibility is 45° to the left and to the right when viewed in a direction at right angles to the longitudinal axis of the vehicle. If the light is fitted within 1m from the rear of the vehicle it may be red in colour or, if the trailer was manufactured before 1 October 1990, it may be white when viewed from the front and red when viewed from the rear.

Numberplates

All trailers must display a numberplate bearing the registration mark of the towing vehicle. The numberplate must show yellow reflective material with black characters. Any number-plate first made from 1st September 2001 **must bear the British Standard No. BS AU 145d and the maker's name, trademark or other means of identification and the suppliers name and postcode. Note!** *The stick-on type of numberplate with self-adhesive characters does not comply with the new Standard. Check with the maker for confirmation that they can produce a test certificate showing that it complies with the Standard.*

Numberplates can now carry the blue Euroflag emblem, which is acceptable by all EEC Member States in place of the normal GB plate. However a GB plate is still required if you travel outside the EEC.

Vehicle marking regulations

If you use a trailer to sell food or ice cream the trailer must display the name and address of the person running the business.

Long vehicle rear markers
These are not required on Type 01 and 02 trailers and are illegal if fitted to trailers being towed by a vehicle with a GVW up to 3,500kg. However, you can and are advised to fit, a rear marker to a trailer, which has a GVW under 3,500kg, when towed by a vehicle with a GVW in excess of 7,500kg.

The 'A'-frame and towing dolly

An 'A'-frame or a dolly can only, legally, be used by a recovery vehicle operator to retrieve a broken-down vehicle and move it to a place of safety. **Note: They cannot be used for any other purpose, including transportation.**

An 'A'-frame is a device that is coupled to a towball and then directly attached to the front of a car to tow that car running on its own wheels. A trailer is defined in the *Road Vehicles (Construction & Use) Regulations 1986* as 'a vehicle drawn by a motor vehicle' so a car being towed becomes, in law, a trailer. It must, therefore, conform fully to those parts of the regulations that apply to a trailer including lighting e.g. triangular reflectors must be fitted.

A Treales Trailers 'Stowboy' towing dolly.

If an 'A'-frame were used without providing any means of braking then the car being towed would be regarded as an unbraked trailer and must, therefore, have a maximum GVW of 750kg. This weight is often wrongly referred to as the actual or kerb weight but it is the towed car's GVW that has to be used. You will not find a car made today with a GVW of less than 750kg. The small Smart Fortwo coupé car, for example, has a GVW of 990kg.

'A'-frames are available with an overrun coupling fitted. These have a cable system that runs from the coupling and into the car via an open window or in some cases through a hole drilled in the car's bulkhead. The cable is attached to the car's brake pedal which provides some braking power, but this would be limited. The majority of cars have brakes operated via a servo, which boosts the performance, but this is only operative when the car's engine is running. Trailer brakes must meet European directives and a car braking system does not meet these with regard to automatic reversing requirements. If you decide to use an 'A' frame to tow a car and the design of 'A' frame uses brackets that are permanently attached to the car then you should notify your insurance company. They would regard these brackets as a modification to the car and you must notify them to avoid any possible problems with a claim following an accident. You should also check with the manufacturer of the 'A' frame that fitting such brackets has the approval of the car manufacturer as these brackets might affect the crumple zone of the car's bodywork.

A towing dolly is really a small trailer with either a straight or vee-shaped drawbar, which has a pair of ramps fitted. A car can then be moved up the ramps so that its front wheels sit over the dolly's axle. The car can then be secured on to the dolly and towed with its back wheels running on the road.

A towing dolly has to conform to all C&U and lighting regulations. They are available in both unbraked and braked versions. The same problems as mentioned above with regard to the use of 'A'-frames also apply to a dolly. You can buy a version with automatic reversing overrun brakes fitted to the axle and a linkage can be connected to the car's brakes, but the same interpretation of the regulations can be applied here.

When a car is placed on the dolly you are then towing two 'trailers' at the same time. Other regulations (the Road Traffic Act) therefore apply, limiting the speed to 40mph on a motorway and 30mph on all other roads. This

The legal way to tow a car behind a motorhome.

used to be 20mph but was changed by the introduction of SI2003 No. 1998.

You will often see these devices being used to tow a car behind a motorhome, but the only way to tow a car legally is to use a car transporter. These can be bought tailor-made for small cars.

Towing cars using an 'A'-frame or a dolly is regarded as a very grey area in law and it will take an Appeal Court case to get a definitive interpretation of the law. If you have any doubts about towing using these devices contact the Primary Safety Branch of the Department for Transport, Great Minster House, Marsham Street, London or check website www.dft.gov.uk for their current advice.

Driving licences

The changes in the regulations introduced on 1 January 1997 were made to bring the UK in line with EEC regulations. These have, however, caused some confusion. If you passed your driving test before that date your licence will cover you for Categories B, C1, D1, B+E, C1+E, D1+E and other Categories F, K, L (electric vehicles), N and P.

If you passed your test after that date you can still tow trailers with your Category B licence without taking a towing test, within certain conditions. These are shown below in Category B:

Throughout these regulations there is used the term 'MAM'. This means maximum authorised mass and in relation to vehicles has the same meaning as 'maximum permissible weight' in *s.108 (1) of the Road Traffic Act 1988*, and in relation to any other vehicle or trailer as maximum gross weight (GVW) in *Regulation 3(2) of the Road Vehicles (Construction and Use) Regulations 1986*.

Driving licence categories and their relevance to trailer use are as follows.

Category A

Motorcycle but excluding vehicles in Category K (other categories covered: B1, K and P).

Motorcycles with an engine over 125cc can tow a trailer with a MAM of maximum 150kg; a maximum width of 1m and the distance from the spindle of the motorcycle's rear wheel to the rear of the trailer is a maximum of 2.5m.

Category B

Motor vehicle other than a vehicle included in categories A, F or P, having a MAM up to 3.5 tonnes and not more than nine seats (including the driver), including:

- A combination of such a vehicle and a trailer where the trailer has a MAM not exceeding 750kg giving a combined MAM (gross train weight) of 4,250kg, *or*
- A vehicle and trailer combination where the trailer's MAM (GVW) does not exceed the car's *kerb weight* and the total MAM does not exceed 3,500kg (other categories covered: F, K and P). **Note:** The total MAM is the car's maximum laden weight, *not the kerb weight*, added to the trailer's GVW.

Drive a large 4x4?
Passed your test after
1 Jan 1997?
This is the size of
trailer you can tow.
Nothing heavier.

Category B1
Sub-category of Category B comprising motor vehicle with three or four wheels, an unladen weight of up to 550kg, a maximum design speed exceeding 50kmh (30mph) and, if fitted with an internal combustion engine, the cubic capacity exceeds 50cc (other categories covered: K and P).

Category B+E
A combination of a motor vehicle and trailer where the motor vehicle is in category B but the combination does not fall within that category (see note under Category B).

Category C
Goods vehicle exceeding 3,500kg MAM (other than a vehicle in Category D, F, G or H), including such a vehicle towing a trailer not exceeding 750kg MAM.

Category C1
A sub-category of Category C comprising a vehicle exceeding 3,500kg but not exceeding 7,500kg MAM, including such a vehicle towing a trailer not exceeding 750kg MAM.

Category C+E (see note 2 below)
Combination of a goods vehicle and trailer where the goods vehicle is in Category C but the combination does not fall within that category (having C+E automatically covers for category B+E).

Category C1+E (see note 3 opposite)
A sub-category of Category C+E comprising any combination of motor vehicle and trailer where:

- The motor vehicle is in sub-category C1.
- The trailer exceeds 750kg MAM but does not exceed the unladen weight of the towing vehicle.
- The combination does not exceed 12,000kg max (having C1+E automatically covers for Category B+E). *If you passed your test before 1 January 1997 you are limited to a vehicle combination of 8,250kg.*

Note: Although the wording is 'any combination' the Police use the formula of adding the MAM of each vehicle together irrespective of the actual weights you may be using. For example, if you passed your test before 1997 the total MAM allowed is 8,250kg. Say you use a 7,000kg truck and have a trailer with a plated MAM of 2,000kg but only load it to 1,250kg to give you a total of 8,250kg you are breaking the law. The police would say that you were operating at 9,000kg (7,000kg truck MAM + 2,000kg trailer MAM) and therefore needed a Category C+E licence.

Category D
Passenger carrying vehicle having more than nine seats (including the driver) including such a vehicle towing a trailer not exceeding 750kg MAM.

Category D1 (see note 1 opposite)
A sub-category of Category D being a passenger-carrying vehicle having more than nine but less than 17 seats, including the driver, including such a vehicle towing a trailer not exceeding 750kg MAM.

Category D+E

The combination of a passenger-carrying vehicle and trailer where the passenger vehicle is on Category D but the combination does not fall within that category (having D+E automatically covers for B+E).

Category D1+E (see note 1 below)

A sub-category of D+E comprising any combination of a motor vehicle and trailer where:
- The motor vehicle is in sub-category D1.
- The trailer exceeds 750kg MAM but not the unladen weight of the towing vehicle.
- The combination does not exceed 12 tonnes MAM, and
- the trailer does not carry passengers.

Category F

Agriculture or forestry tractor, other than a vehicle in Category H (other categories covered: K).

Category G

Road roller.

Category H

Track-laying vehicle steered by its tracks.

Category K

Mowing machine or pedestrian controlled vehicle.

Category P

Moped.

NOTES:

The following refer to licences/entitlements issued before 1 January 1997.

1 Limited to driving vehicles not used for 'hire or reward'.
2 Entitlement may be claused 'limited to drawbar trailer combinations'.
3 Limited to combinations not exceeding 8,250kg MAM.

> ## Info
>
> In the official driving licence legislation the term tonnes is used e.g. 8.25tonnes. A tonne is 1,000kg. An imperial ton is 1,016kg.

Speed limits

When towing with a car, passenger-carrying vehicle, car-derived van or dual-purpose vehicle the speed limits are as follows:

- Motorways 60mph.
- Dual carriageways 60mph, unless a lower limit is in force.
- Other roads 50mph, unless a lower limit is in force.

When towing with a goods vehicle between 3.5 and 7.5 tonnes:

- Motorways 60mph
- Dual carriageways 60mph, unless a lower limit is in force.
- Other roads 50mph, unless a lower limit is in force.

Note: *Only applies where the aggregate maximum laden weight of vehicle and trailer is not more than 7,500kg.*

When towing with a large goods vehicle (LGV) exceeding 7.5 tonnes:

- Motorways 60mph.
- Dual carriageways 50mph, unless a lower limit is in force.
- Other roads 40mph, unless a lower limit is in force

Tachographs

If you have a vehicle that has a GVW exceeding 3,500kg it will have a tachograph fitted to conform to the law. If your vehicle has a GVW not exceeding 3,500kg then hitching a trailer up to it may bring you into the scope of the Drivers Hours Regulations. If the towing vehicle has a GTW exceeding 3,500kg and the combined gross weights of the vehicle and trailer also exceed 3,500kg then a tachograph is required. If the outfit is being used for commercial use and you are not towing a trailer that is exempt from the regulations (see below) then you will need to have a tachograph fitted and must use it when towing.

Changes in the *Drivers Hours Regulations* have caused considerable controversy. Many people believe that they are now required to fit a tachograph when towing a trailer. Some newspapers have misinformed readers by reporting that small vehicles such as Ford Fiesta vans need one when towing, this is untrue.

The tachograph regulations in *The Transport Act 1968 Pt VI* prior to August 1, 1998 referred to 'goods vehicles' so at that time cars and dual-purpose vehicles were exempt. The changes introduced the wording 'any vehicles used to carry goods'. This is the wording used in *EC Regulations 3820/85* and *3821/85* and the UK

> ## Info
>
> **Note:**
> Motorhomes, although built on a commercial vehicle chassis, normally of a Category N1 vehicle, are reclassified in law as passenger-carrying vehicles of Category M1. This means that they are subjected to passenger car speed limits for GVWs up to 3,500kg. If they have a GVW exceeding that figure they come under the speed limits for a LGV.

Government say that they are simply bringing UK Regulations into line. Obviously a car can be used to carry goods hence the considerable confusion caused by this wording.

An Appeal Court case (Laverick and Clarke v Wilmot, Chief Constable) in July 1998 established a legal interpretation of 'maximum permissible weight'. Previously the Police simply added together the maximum permissible weight of the towing vehicle to that of the trailer irrespective of whether any load was being carried and if the total exceeded 3,500kg and the journey was commercial then a tachograph was required.

In this case the towing vehicle had a GTW of 3,500kg but the sum of the GVWs was over 3,500kg, therefore, in the view of the Police a tachograph should have been fitted and used. The actual weight of the outfit was measured

A Siemens VDO analogue tachograph combined with the speedometer.

and found to be below 3,500kg so was within the vehicle's GTW. The appeal was won on the fact that exceeding the vehicles GTW would have been an offence of having an overloaded vehicle.

This case established the requirement for the Police to look at the GTW of the towing vehicle and they have to take the lower of the two ways of calculating the weights. As most cars and car-derived vans have a GTW lower than 3,500kg they can never require a tachograph.

For example, a Ford Mondeo 2.0i has a Gross Train Weight of 2,800kg and can tow trailers commercially and never require a tachograph. If this GTW was exceeded an offence would be committed of using an overloaded vehicle, but not of breaking tachograph laws.

If you tow a trailer as part of your business you will, therefore, have to look at your choice of towing vehicle carefully. A Land Rover Discovery, depending on a particular model's kerb weight, can tow a trailer with a GVW of around 1,500kg whereas a Land Rover Freelander can tow around 2,000kg before a tachograph is required. Some large cars can bring you into scope of the tachograph requirements so check the handbook before buying. See also Chapter Five, *Preparing your car for towing*, and Chapter Six, *Fitting a Towbar*.

There are of course exemptions and the ones that are of most concern to light trailer users are as follows:

■ vehicle combinations being used for the non-commercial carriage of goods for personal use; any vehicle (including goods) not exceeding 3,500kg maximum permissible weight (including any trailer);

■ vehicles used for the carriage of passengers constructed or equipped to carry not more than 17 persons including the driver. If going abroad the EC Regulations restrict this exemption to nine seats including the driver;

■ vehicles undergoing road tests for technical development, repair or maintenance purposes and new or rebuilt vehicles which are not yet in service;

■ vehicles being used by agricultural, horticultural, forestry or fishery undertakings to carry goods within a 50km (31 mile) radius of the place where they are normally based, including local administrative areas the centres of which are situated within that radius. Where fishery undertakings are concerned this only applies to the carriage of live fish, or a catch of fish from the place of landing to the place where it is to be processed;

■ vehicles carrying animal waste or carcasses which are not intended for human consumption;

■ vehicles carrying live animals between a farm and a local market or from a local market to a local slaughterhouse. If you travel long distance to either sell or buy livestock you would require a tachograph to be fitted and used if your vehicle combination falls within the scope of the Regulations even travelling without a load;

■ vehicles being used as shops at a local market; for door-to-door selling; mobile banking, exchange or savings transactions; for worship, for the lending of books, records or cassettes; for cultural events or

exhibitions. Note: such vehicles must be specially fitted for the use in question;

- a vehicle carrying goods having a permissible maximum weight not exceeding 7.5 tonnes and carrying material or equipment for the driver's use in the course of his work within a 50km (31 mile) radius of the place where the vehicle is normally based and providing driving the vehicle is not the driver's main activity;
- vehicles operating exclusively on an island not exceeding 2,300 square kilometres in area and which is not connected to the rest of Great Britain by a bridge, ford or tunnel. This includes the Isle of Wight, Arran and Bute;
- a vehicle being used for driving instruction with a view to obtaining a driving licence. Note: this does not apply if the vehicle or any trailer attached to it is carrying goods on a journey for hire or reward, or for or in any connection with any trade.

Please take care regarding specific plant and equipment trailers e.g. mobile generators or air compressors. These have always been regarded as exempt from the regulations as they are not built to carry goods but in a recent Court case involving a mobile gantry it was found that this type of trailer fell within the scope of the Tachograph regulations. This may go to appeal so please check with the Department for Transport, for the latest situation regarding the need for a Tachograph if you will be towing trailers such as these.

In May 2006 a new type of tachograph is being introduced, a digital electronic version. This has been developed to overcome the fraudulent use that has occurred with the analogue type tachographs. This will apply throughout the EEC.

For a good source of frequently asked questions regarding drivers' hours you can obtain a free copy of the DfT's *Drivers' Hours* handbook GV262 from your nearest Large

Goods Vehicle test centre. Look under Vehicle & Operator Services Agency (VOSA) in your local telephone directory for the number. You can now download the handbook from the DfT website as well as the frequently asked questions relating to drivers' hours. See: http://www.dft.gov.uk/stellent/groups/dft_freight/documents/page/dft_freight_504543.pdf

Operators' licences

The police may tell you that if you have a tachograph fitted to your towing vehicle that you then require an operators' licence. This is not necessarily so. Operators' licensing is governed by *The Goods Vehicles (Licensing of Operators) Act 1995, The Goods Vehicles (Licensing of Operators) Regulations 1995 (SI 1995 No. 2869)* and *The Goods Vehicles (Licensing of Operators) (Fees) Regulations 1995 (SI 1995 No. 3000)*.

Subject to certain exemptions (see below) operators' licensing applies to all goods vehicles and vehicle combinations used for the carriage of goods in connection with trade or business and which exceed 3.5 tonnes gross plated weight or, if unplated but fitted with power brakes 1,525kg unladen weight. Any trailer, with a GVW in excess of 3,500kg but an unladen weight of not more than 1,020kg unladen being discounted.

The following exemptions would apply to light trailer use:
- Dual-purpose vehicles and trailers towed thereby,
- passenger vehicles and any trailer towed, when being so used.

Carriage of animals

If you transport horses or livestock by trailer you must comply with the relevant laws covering the welfare of the animals. The current law is the *Welfare of Animals (Transport) Order 1997 (Statutory Instrument 1997 No. 1480)* and amending legislation. If you require more information it can be obtained by looking at website http://www.defra.gov.uk/ or by contacting your local Trading Standards Department, as they enforce this law.

The law is likely to change by 2007 following a new European directive giving more space requirements for the animals. This will apply to the carriage of animals for business purposes.

A Siemens VDO digital tachograph.

BUYING AND HIRING A TRAILER

So you are thinking of buying a trailer – how should you go about it? First, simple as it may sound, decide what type of trailer you need.

As you have seen in Chapter 1, the range of trailers is enormous so you must analyse your requirements to start narrowing down the choice to just a few models. Ask yourself the following questions:

- What do I need the trailer to do?
- Where am I going to keep it?
- What can my car pull?

These are just a few of the things to be determined before going out to buy a trailer.

Vehicle towing capacity

A most important fact to determine is your vehicle's towing capacity. This can be found by looking at the VIN plate under the bonnet or in the owner's manual. If there are discrepancies between figures on the plate and the manual, either work to the lower figure or refer back to the car dealer or manufacturer for clarification. The information is usually given as the maximum permissible weight for

A typical VIN plate, normally found on the engine compartment bulkhead of the car or on the driver's door pillar. The weights show (from the top): maximum permitted mass, gross train weight, maximum front axle load, and maximum rear axle load.

unbraked trailers and then for trailers with brakes.

It is an offence under the Road Traffic Act 1988 to tow a trailer exceeding the car's maximum towing limit and should you be unfortunate enough to be involved in an accident while doing so you could find that your insurance policy is invalid. This could be a very expensive mistake to make.

Now that you know what you can pull you can start to look at trailers. These fall into two categories – braked and unbraked. Taking unbraked trailers first, many people think they can tow up to a maximum of 750kg, but unless you have a very large car you will find that you cannot take this weight as you can only tow up to half your car's unladen weight ('kerb weight').

To give an example, if you had a Ford Scorpio you could tow around 750kg (depending on the specific model), but a Ford Focus would only tow around 550kg. This is a sensible ruling, as your car's brakes have to take into account an extra 50% weight burden. In addition, you do not want the 'tail wagging the dog' scenario with the trailer trying to take over.

Don't forget that the weights shown are inclusive of the unladen weight of the trailer. All unbraked trailers have to have a manufacturer's plate mounted on the nearside of the drawbar giving the unladen and maximum permitted weights and – from 1 January 1997 – the year of manufacture. Look at these carefully before buying.

Unbraked trailers

If it is an unbraked trailer you want to buy some types are designed to stand on end, thus reducing their storage space requirement.

On the other hand, your trailer may have to be stored out of doors. If so, a galvanised trailer would be advisable. As regards the type, ask yourself:

- Do I just require a normal trailer with shallow sides?
- What is the largest item I will carry?
- Therefore, what size trailer do I need?
- Will I require a drop-down tailboard for easier loading and unloading? It makes it so much easier when carrying products such as sand or gravel.
- Will the load be damaged if I tow in the rain?
- If so, then I will need a cover.
- Should this be a canvas one or a rigid lid? All variations are available.

If you like the 'great outdoors' you may use the trailer for all your camping gear. Perhaps you are considering a trailer tent as these are usually built on unbraked chassis and are innovatively designed.

When buying an unbraked trailer it should be fitted with a secondary coupling – usually a chain or a cable. This is law on all trailers sold new from 1 January 1997, and this secondary coupling must be used when towing. It is designed to retain the trailer and keep it from hitting the ground if the trailer were to become detached from the towing vehicle. However, it is not recommended that the secondary coupling be looped around the ball. Some towbars have provision for attaching a secondary coupling to a 'pigtail' but many are not so equipped, but you can purchase a bolt-on pigtail which should be fitted to the reverse side of one of the towball bolts.

To make the attachment you simply put one of the links in the chain over the end of the pigtail and pass the chain along the spiral to its inner end. Select a link that allows sufficient articulation of the trailer but would prevent the trailer coupling hitting the road surface if it becomes detached from the car. If the remaining length of chain is hanging down simply put another of the links over the end of the pigtail, pass it along the spiral to take up the free length.

Alternatively, if the towbar has a bracket with a hole for a breakaway cable you can use a suitably robust 'D' shackle. Some owners even use a padlock for this but it must be of good quality.

Lightweight trailers do not normally come with a jockey wheel, they simply have a skid plate under the drawbar to keep the coupling head off the ground when the trailer is parked. You may prefer to have a jockey wheel fitted.

Above: An unbraked trailer like this Erdé can be stood on its end, thereby saving storage space.

Far left: A flexible PVC top and drop-down tailboard are handy items to have on a small trailer like this.

Left: A Conway trailer tent

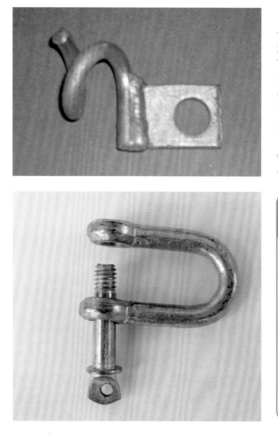

For all round satisfactory performance when towing, the recommendation of not exceeding 85% of your car's kerb weight is a good one. This is endorsed by the National Caravan Council (NCC), the Caravan Club, the Camping and Caravanning Club, the Department for Transport (DfT), and the Driving Standards Agency (DSA). Copies of the *Caravan Towing Code,* priced £2.95 at the time of writing, are available from the National Caravan Council.

Tip

The *Caravan Towing Code* is the caravan industry's definitive guide to towing and is supported by the Caravan Club and the Camping and Caravanning Club.

It contains recommendations reviewed and agreed by the former Department of Environment, Transport and the Regions (now the DfT) and the Driving Standards Agency. Essential reading whether you're a beginner or already well experienced in towing.

This is helpful, for example, when car access is limited. If you do not have a jockey wheel, it is recommended that you put the load in the trailer when the trailer is hooked up to the car, otherwise, you may find you cannot physically lift the laden trailer onto the towball.

Braked trailers

If you need to tow more than half your car's kerb weight you will have to buy a braked trailer. These are available in both single, tandem and tri-axle versions, with single axles going up to 1,800kg maximum permissible weight and tandem/tri-axles up to a maximum of 3,500kg. Obviously, your car's maximum towing limit will determine the weight of the trailer you can consider.

Tip

If you do have problems lifting the coupling with reasonable ease then the trailer load is too far forward and needs to be re-distributed. Keep the heaviest part of the load over the axle.

Be careful if you passed your driving test after 1 January 1997 and have only a category B licence. This only allows you to tow a braked trailer with a maximum permissible weight not exceeding your car's kerb weight providing that the car's maximum authorised mass (note, not kerb weight) when added to the trailer's maximum permitted weight does not exceed 3,500kg. If you want to tow a trailer that is heavier than the car or the combined weights exceed 3,500kg then you will have to take and pass the B+E towing test.

The braked class of trailer comes with two body widths, either between the wheels or over the wheels. This obviously affects the loading height or the space utilisation of the trailer. A box van trailer, for example, with a body built between the wheels will have a perfectly rectangular floor whereas one with the bodywork over the wheels will have wheelarches intruding into the body space. This could cause problems with some loads but you do gain a lot more space. To get a perfectly flat floor it would have to be built over the wheels, giving an increase in the loading height of between 220mm and 370mm depending on the tyre specifications. This means that the centre of gravity is higher so you must take this into account when towing. A higher centre of gravity can mean that the trailer leans over more when cornering and can give more severe pitching at the towbar. Reduce cornering speed to lessen this effect.

The brakes fitted to this category of trailer are of the overrun type. What this means is that when you apply the brakes in your car the trailer tries to catch up or 'overrun' the car. This action pushes the coupling drawshaft through the body of the overrun device and operates the brakes by a lever connected to the brake linkage. This movement is controlled by a hydraulic damper, which gives progressive braking. Hydraulically damped designs were introduced in the 1960s and were initially used on caravans before being introduced on trailers. Before their introduction the movement was controlled by a coil spring.

Spring couplings are still to be seen on older trailers but do not provide very good braking. The overrun device had a short travel, in the order of 25mm, against spring pressure to apply the brakes, so they were not very progressive. As the spring became weaker with use you could say that the brakes were either on or off with not much in-between. The introduction of a hydraulic damper instead of a spring gave much better control of the trailer brakes because it created a longer stroke, typically around 100mm.

Brakes on trailers made since October 1988 must be of the automatic reversing type. This means that when a trailer is reversed the brakes do not come on with sufficient force to prevent you reversing. Older trailers and caravans with either hydraulically damped or spring couplings were fitted with a reversing brake lever to stop the brakes being applied when reversing. This is fiddly to use and means getting out of the car to engage the lever – if you have to ease forward during the manoeuvre the lever would automatically disengage and necessitates getting out again. To overcome this, some manufacturers supplied electrical solenoid devices to hold the reverse lever in place. Even these were awkward to use, as you had to move the car backwards and forwards to get the drawshaft in the correct position to work. Some owners would use a spring or a rubber band made from an old inner tube to hold the lever back. The only problem was that they could then drive forwards on their journey, forgetting to free

the spring or rubber band and then the trailer brakes would not work!

You can see, therefore, why the introduction of automatic reversing brakes was so welcome. Hydraulically damped overrun devices became mandatory in October 1982, but you can still buy spring couplings to replace existing worn out ones on earlier trailers. The type of coupling can give you a good indication of the age of an old trailer.

Suspension types

The type of suspension should be taken into consideration when buying a trailer. Each type has its own characteristics and one type may be better than others for your needs. There are two main groups of materials used for the suspension of trailers – rubber or steel. Rubber is used in compression, shear or tension, and steel in leaf, coil or torsion bar forms.

RUBBER SUSPENSION SYSTEMS
Rubber suspension in tension is found on small, unbraked, trailers and takes the form of large rubber bands. Although it looks primitive and fragile, this system is surprisingly effective.

However, most small trailers use rubber in compression. The main axle tube is square and bolted straight to the chassis frame. A square bar is inserted into the axle tube at 45°, to which the drop arm and stub axle are fitted. The four triangular spaces left in the corners of the axle tube are filled with circular rubber inserts. When a road wheel hits a bump the drop arm moves up rotating the inner square bar and compresses the rubber inserts. This design is known as the Neidhart type after its originator.

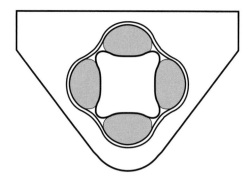

Although this design can be used on larger trailers up to 3,500kg for many applications a better ride quality is sought, with greater wheel movement, so a number of companies have developed alternatives to this simple square bar using a square tube design.

AL-KO introduced their profiled outer tube with six faces but use only three rubber inserts and a centre bar which has three concave faces. This design gives significant improvements in ride quality as the rubber rolls as well as compresses.

The British company Avonride, stayed with four rubber inserts but put large radii on the corners of the tube and used a profiled inner bar giving a cam effect. This 'S'-type axle certainly gives a better ride than their standard 'N'-type axle with a normal square inner bar.

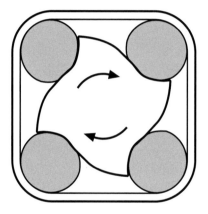

Indespension also stayed with four rubber inserts, but chose to profile the inner bar with four concave faces as well as to profile the outer tube accordingly.

AL-KO Kober axle.

Rubber can also be used in shear and this can be found on Peak Trailer axles in two forms. The Flexiride has the rubber fully bonded to both the inner bar and the outer housing. Due to the production process this design is supplied in paired units as opposed to a complete axle.

For a complete axle, there is the Bramberide suspension unit, where the inner shaft has square section rubber elements bonded on and is then pressed into the axle tube.

The German axle manufacturer Knott, supply a rubber torsion axle where the inner shaft and the axle tube are circular with the rubber bonded in between. The benefit claimed for rubber in torsion is that there is no movement between the rubber and metal components, thus reducing wear and giving longer life and quiet running.

It is rare in the UK to find rubber suspensions fitted with hydraulic dampers (also known as shock absorbers), the theory being that rubber has its own inherent damping characteristics allied to the fact that our road surfaces are, in general, quite good in

Peak Bramberide suspension units.

STEEL SUSPENSION SYSTEMS

The most commonly found steel suspension design consists of a traditional beam axle and leaf spring. Although many people look on this system as old-fashioned it has been refined over the years and gives a very reliable working life with good ride qualities, especially when transporting livestock.

The largest UK trailer manufacturer, Ifor Williams Trailers, uses this design on all its braked axles. The springs can be replaced if required – unlike rubber suspensions where the whole axle has to be returned to the maker for repair. There is some damping in this design as a result of friction between the individual leaves of the springs, but improvements in ride and braking would come from the fitment of hydraulic dampers.

You may also come across coil spring suspensions on older trailers, but these designs were superseded by the lower cost rubber designs. They were mainly used on caravan chassis. Indeed, some older trailers are simply rebodied caravan chassis. The main makers were B&B Trailers, with a semi-trailing arm design; Peak Trailers, with a swing axle design, and Caravans International, with a trailing arm

comparison with other parts of Europe. The fitment of dampers certainly improves both the ride and the braking performance due to keeping the tyre contact patch (the area of tread that touches the road surface) constant. This area can change considerably with the reduced load on the tyre if the wheel is lifting or skipping on the road surface thus increasing the stopping distance. Many axles are supplied with the necessary brackets to allow dampers to be fitted. Trailers used on the Continent often have dampers fitted as standard. Bear this in mind when determining the specification of your trailer if you are going to carry any fragile loads

design. The first two systems encroached on the wheelbox space and were heavy, but gave a superb ride. It is interesting to note that the German trailer manufacturer Westfalia, still uses coil spring suspensions.

The other steel suspension is the torsion bar design. The principle here is to have the suspension drop arm connected to the outer end of the torsion bar with the inner end anchored in the axle tube. When the wheel hits a bump the torsion bar is twisted, giving progressive suspension. The torsion bars can be either a round bar or more commonly, laminated from steel strips, which is really a flat leaf spring, but instead of being deflected by a vertical load it is twisted by the load. Friction damping applies to the leaves but again, hydraulic dampers are required. Steel torsion bar suspensions are not in common use now on trailers due to their cost but are still employed in the caravan industry by the German Hobby Group.

Which suspension system you choose depends on your individual requirements and your budget, with the rubber-in-compression type being the cheapest and the steel torsion bar the dearest.

You should now be in a position to establish the ideal specification for your trailer and can decide whether to buy new or used.

Hiring before you buy

It is a good idea, before buying a trailer, to hire one of a similar specification. In this way you can ensure this is the specification you want as trailer hire charges are relatively modest, and in addition, some hire companies will help with the provision of boxes, packing materials etc.

When you are hiring a trailer you must be aware of the insurance situation. Many hirers will offer full insurance cover as part of the hire

Above and left: Typical signs of heavy-duty use of a hire trailer include damage to fairings and wheelarches, as here. Make sure the hire company is aware of these before you commence your hire, or you could find yourself facing a repair bill for damage you haven't done!

fee, or at an extra cost but not all do this and in which case you will carry full responsibility for the trailer while it is hired out to you. In addition you should contact your car insurers to see if they will provide cover while you are towing. You could also approach your household insurers to see if they will provide cover when the trailer is not being towed.

You will have to use any security devices, such as wheel clamps and hitchlocks, supplied with the trailer when not using it, failure to do so will invalidate any insurance policies.

Read the hire agreement carefully before signing, noting especially any items regarding instructions in the use of the trailer, before driving away. It is your responsibility to return the trailer at the agreed time, or you will incur penalty charges. The trailer must be returned in a clean condition or you will be charged a cleaning fee to ensure the trailer is suitable for the next hirer. You should also inspect the trailer before hiring to see if there is any damage. If there is, make sure that it is noted on the hire form. The hirer will check the trailer on return to see if there is any fresh damage. Not surprisingly, a deposit will be required on hiring to cover for damage or a late return. All hire fees are payable before leaving and the deposit will be refunded on your return.

You will need to produce your driving licence and one other form of identification, such as a

utility bill, bank statement or similar which bears your name and address. You will also be asked for your business telephone number. This is necessary on account of trailer theft and your visit may be recorded on a video tape or your photograph taken digitally.

Hiring a trailer can show you if your car is compatible with different types of suspensions and how it handles and performs while towing. This is a great help in making sure that you buy the best trailer for your needs.

Buying – new or second-hand?

If your budget allows, buy new. You will be getting a product that is made to the latest standards, usually with a fully galvanised chassis and a manufacturer's guarantee. There will be a trailer centre in your area that will sell all sizes of trailer – look in *Yellow Pages* or similar directories under 'Trailer Manufactures and Suppliers' and 'Trailer Hire'.

The smallest unbraked trailers are also available from Halfords, caravan dealers and other car spares outlets as well as by mail order. These are normally for self-assembly, as can be seen in Chapter 4, or they are supplied ready assembled.

Buying – from a dealer or privately?

If you are buying second-hand you will need to decide whether to purchase from a dealer or privately. Normally a dealer will have checked a trailer, put right any faults and a guarantee will be provided. However, the price is usually higher. Typically, it is less expensive when dealing with a private vendor but you must ensure that you are not buying a stolen trailer. If you are responding to a newspaper advertisement by telephone simply ask: 'Have you sold the trailer?' The vendor may have more than one tucked away. If he answers: 'Which trailer?' you will know the likely situation.

When buying a pre-owned trailer always ask for the details shown on the chassis plate, requesting the maker's name, the chassis number and the unladen and gross weights. If the vendor cannot supply this and says that there isn't a plate, assume that the trailer might be stolen. Do not consider buying trailers under these circumstances as they may have a hidden electronic tag fitted which

may be found during a police roadside check. You would then lose the trailer and have no means of getting your money back.

Be prepared to travel to the vendor's house and ask if the original purchase receipt is available. If the vendor suggests meeting you halfway at a convenient pub or cafe, do not agree to this. If the only telephone number you have is a mobile one be wary. If you definitely have suspicions about the offer, why not inform your local police station? Ask them to ring the advertiser to see if they feel that it is worth investigating. They might be pleased to follow it up. You may, alternatively, be in the position of having a trailer stolen yourself and would welcome the police finding it for you.

What to look for

When you have located a trailer that is worth inspecting there are many pitfalls to look out for. For example, how old is the trailer? Unfortunately, unlike cars, trailers do not have their own registration number so you cannot look at a numberplate for the age identifier. The requirement for unbraked trailers to have

the year of manufacture displayed only came in on 1 January 1997. At the time of writing there is, surprisingly, no legal requirement for braked trailers to have the date of manufacture marked on them.

The easiest way of getting an indication of the age of a braked trailer is to look at the overrun coupling.

- Is it the old spring coupling mentioned previously? If so it must have been made before October 1982.
- If it has a hydraulically damped coupling but not auto reversing brakes it could have been made anywhere between 1965 and October 1988.
- If it has auto-reversing brakes it will have been made since October 1988.

Needless to say, there is no way of knowing how many miles a trailer has done. All you can do is check over the trailer, looking for wear and tear. Start at the front and work through to the back looking first at the coupling head and overrun device.

If possible, take a new towball with you and insert it into the coupling head.

Alternatively, ask to couple up the trailer to your car.

- Check to see if it is a good fit with little play.
- Does the automatic locking system retain the coupling head or can it be prised from the ball. The easy way to check is to use the jockey wheel, if fitted, and try to lift the back of the car.
- Many coupling heads have wear indicators either by means of markings on the side or with buttons at the front of the head. What do these display? Do they show that you are within the wear tolerance limits?

With the trailer off the car:

- Pull the head upward to check for wear in the drawshaft. If there is noticeable movement the bearings are worn and these can only be replaced by the manufacturer.
- Try pushing the coupling head into the overrun device – the movement should be steady with some resistance and then it should return itself. If it does not move or moves with little or no resistance the damper has failed and requires replacement.

up the opposite side of the trailer putting an axle stand under the axle.

- With the handbrake off and wearing industrial or gardening gloves, run your hands around the tyre to see if there are any bulges in the tread or tyre wall. If you find any, the tyre will need replacing.
- Check the tread for wear and the sidewalls for cracks. Trailer tyres generally do not wear out the tread before the need to change them. Most trailers don't actually cover lots of miles, but they can be left standing for long periods.
- Check the markings on the tyre and see that the correct specification is fitted. (See Appendix B) It is not uncommon to find that incorrect tyres are fitted as they are often of the same size as cars but need a stronger casing – usually a 'C' rating. If it is a single-axle trailer, bear in mind that only two wheels are carrying the same weight as the four on the car so stronger tyres are required.
- Check the age of the tyre from the date code moulded on the side walls of the tyre. Do not use a tyre that is seven or more years old. They should preferably be changed at five

- Apply the handbrake and push the trailer forwards to see if the trailer can be moved. If the trailer is fitted with automatic reversing brakes push it in the reverse direction; it may move a short distance before the stored energy system applies more power to the brakes. If it does not hold, either the system is out of adjustment or the shoes are worn.
- Inspect the tyres. First chock one of the wheels to stop the trailer moving. Now jack

BRMA car tyre sidewall drawing. (Reproduced with kind permission of the British Rubber Manufacturers' Association).

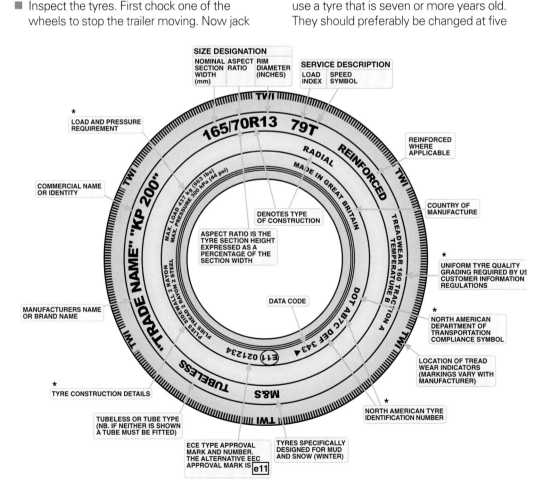

years up to seven years regardless of how much tread is left.

- Next, grasp the top of the wheel and pull it towards you. Is there noticeable movement? If there is, prise off the axle cap and look at the retaining nut. If it is fitted with a split pin it means that taper roller bearings are be fitted and the play can be taken up with adjustment. If there is a plain nut, this means that the bearings are worn and require replacement. Spin the wheel and listen to see if there is a rumble, proving that the bearings are worn.
- Check, also, to see if the wheel has any run out – that is, any wobble from side to side, as it rotates, that may indicate that it has been 'kerbed'.
- If there is any such movement, you must check that the drop arm of a rubber suspension axle has not been bent – if so, the axle would have to be sent back to the maker for repair. It is not a DIY job.

Now check the other wheels in turn.

- Look under the trailer at the condition of the brake mechanism. Are there signs of grease on the compensators or are they dry or rusty?
- Is the wiring harness clipped tidily with no damage to the insulation?
- Check the condition of the lights. Are any of the lenses cracked?
- Check the operation of the lights when connected to your car.
- Check the chassis for repairs or cracks, especially where the drawbar 'A'-frame meets the first cross member, as this is a critical place for fatigue cracking. Check the bodywork for dents, cuts or other damage. An indicator of heavy use is the droplocks fitted to drop-down tailboards – if there is no part of the slot showing above the cross pin then the trailer has most likely had a hard life. Another element, which reveals that a trailer has been heavily used, is the floor. At best, there may be signs of slight warping, rust or damage where heavy items have been dropped on the floor. For horseboxes, in particular, damage will have been caused by the actions of hooves as well as urine and faeces.

Far left: A droplock in use. Note the gap in the slot above the pin.

Buying price

Unfortunately, there is no published guide to prices for second-hand trailers. You can, however, check out quotes for a similar trailer by telephoning dealers around the country to get an indication of the spread of prices. You can then establish a suitable price to offer. A private seller is often willing to negotiate the price.

MAKING YOUR OWN TRAILER

4

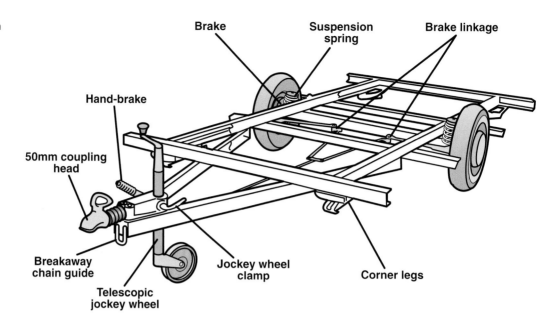

B & B Trailers caravan chassis.

Brake

Suspension spring

Brake linkage

Hand-brake

50mm coupling head

Breakaway chain guide

Telescopic jockey wheel

Jockey wheel clamp

Corner legs

1. From used parts

UNBRAKED

It is many years since you could simply go to a car scrapyard, buy an old car rear axle and use it as the running gear for a home-made trailer. I built my first trailer this way using the rear suspension units from a Bond Minicar. These were the rubber Bramber Flexitor type now made by Peak Trailers (see Chapter 3). I did not require brakes so I used the hubs as unbraked units. You cannot do this now; the law requires that if brakes are fitted 'they must work'. Moreover, car-type brakes do not conform to the European Directive covering trailer brakes as they are not of the automatic reversing type.

BRAKED

If you do need a braked trailer and want to build it yourself, the easiest way is to go to a caravan breaker and buy an old caravan chassis because these have had automatic reversing brakes fitted since the mid-1970s. The only snag is that caravan axles are nearly all wide tracked and cannot be reduced in width if you do not want a wide trailer. Caravan axles were usually made in varying capacities e.g. 900kg, 1,100kg, 1,300kg and 1,500kg in single axle form. The chassis plate should tell you what capacity axles

and brakes are fitted. A search on the Internet or in your local classified directory will give you the location of the nearest caravan breaker. The old British caravan chassis makers – B&B Trailers (semi-trailing arm suspension), Peak Trailers (swing axle suspension) and CI (trailing arm suspension) were all made with automatic reversing brakes and all used coil springs with hydraulic dampers. They make a very good trailer indeed as they were of traditional construction with at least four cross-members making it a simple job in placing trailer bodywork straight on to the chassis. There can be some problems though in obtaining spare parts for older designs of chassis.

The rubber suspension type then took over the market and you will find AL-KO Kober and BPW made the most commonly found designs. Gradually the amount of steel in a chassis was reduced and the chassis now has just two longitudinal members with the axle tube as the only cross-member. This is because caravan floors now take a greater share of the load-bearing construction, being made of a sandwich of foam between two layers of plywood.

BPW caravan chassis.

2. From new parts

UNBRAKED

You can build and tow a trailer with a gross vehicle weight (GVW) of 750kg without brakes, but can only load it up to a maximum weight of half your car's kerb weight. If your car, say, can only tow to a GVW of 500kg it would be better and cheaper to build one using an axle, wheels and tyres suitable for that GVW.

The simplest way would be to buy a 'T' frame drawbar and axle assembly on which you can put any type of body structure that suits your need.

However, this is more expensive than buying separate suspension units which also offer greater scope when establishing the dimensions for the trailer. These are available in various designs using rubber as the suspension medium and are supplied with mounting plates, which are welded to the chassis frame to which the units are then bolted.

Care should be taken when welding these on to ensure that they either 'toe in' or are parallel with the frame. The suspension units can be bolted to the mounting plates, the wheels put on and then they can be clamped to the chassis to give the desired amount of toe-in and then welded into place. Toe in is where the dimension across the front of the trailer wheels is less than that across the back of the wheels i.e. pointing inwards. It is common for the wheels to have no toe-in, i.e. parallel or to toe in by up to 3mm for 13in wheels. Toe-in helps the stability of a trailer at speed.

When designing a trailer the most difficult details to determine are the length of the drawbar and the axle position. A longer drawbar makes the trailer more stable while towing. The longer the distance from the coupling head to the wheel centres, the easier it is to reverse the trailer. The axle position has a significant effect on the nose weight and you should aim for a positive nose weight when the trailer is unladen of around 5–20kg depending on the size of the trailer. When building your own trailer you can determine the axle position by balancing the chassis on supports (axle stands are ideal for this) and measuring the nose weight at different locations by moving the support. Remember that the point on the chassis which gives you the desired nose weight is not the axle mounting position but the centre line of the wheels. The suspension units have a trailing arm so the mounting point will be in front of the axle centre line as the drop arms should face the rear of the trailer. As a rule of thumb the wheel position is

A T-bar chassis. Note the eye coupling.

Pairs of suspension units.

usually around 50–150mm behind the centre line of the trailer's platform or bodywork.

Typical steel sections for a popular size of trailer of 1,200mm x 900mm (4ft x 3ft) (internal body size) would be to use 40 x 40 x 3mm angle section with 50 x 50 x 3mm corner posts. The drawbar would be made from 50 x 50 x 3mm square hollow section tube, the axle from 40 x 40 x 3mm square hollow section tube and the floor reinforcement would use a combination of 25 x 25 x 3mm and 40 x 25 x 3mm angle section. Obviously, for larger trailers much heavier gauge steel would be required.

The drawbar should be level with the ground when the trailer is attached to the car and depending on the wheel and tyre size you have chosen may require a crank in it to lift the coupling head up to align with the towball. The alternative is to mount the suspension units on a sub-frame positioned underneath the main chassis longitudinal members to lift the platform and hence a straight drawbar up to the required height. The towball height should be between 350mm and 420mm from the ground so I would recommend that you aim to have the trailer's drawbar and coupling set at 400mm.

BRAKED

Unless you want a design of trailer that cannot be bought 'off the shelf', it may not be cost-effective to build one from new components. The price that you pay for an axle and a coupling, as a one-off, will be proportionately higher than the cost of equivalent items when incorporated in a factory-built trailer.

If you do want to make your own braked trailer there are a number of decisions that you must make to ensure that the components you buy are the correct ones. Ask yourself:

- What will be the gross vehicle weight of the trailer? Do not forget that this is the weight of the trailer plus its load.
- What will be the overall width and length of the trailer?
- Will the bodywork go between the wheels or over the wheels?
- What wheel and tyre size will be used?
- Will it have a drop-down tailboard and/or ramps?
- Will it need metal or plastic mudguards?
- Will it need propstands?

The actual laden weight of the trailer is limited to the towing capacity of your vehicle. Check your handbook and VIN plate and see what the vehicle can tow. You can then determine the capacity of the coupling, overrun device, axles, brakes and tyres that are needed to comply with the car's towing limit.

Why the need for all these decisions?

If your towing limit is 1,000kg then you look in running gear manufacturers' lists to find the items that can be used at that capacity. This is most likely to be an 1,100kg system. You must buy a coupling, overrun device and braked axle made by the same manufacturer, as they will have been Type Approved as a system combination. Each component will have the Type Approval plates fixed on them showing the maximum capacity of each item. It is essential that you buy the correct capacity of overrun device as they all use a hydraulic damper to control the rate of application of the brakes. There is a range of dampers catering for weights up to a maximum of 3,500kg. Do not make the mistake of asking for a 'heavy duty' overrun device as there is no such thing and you might be sold one with too high a rating. That could happen if the parts salesman at the trailer centre is not experienced. If you buy a unit with, say, a 3,500kg damper and have a trailer with a maximum weight of 1,000kg then it is likely that the brakes will not be applied fully. That's because the force supplied by the weight of the trailer will be insufficient to overcome the damper valve settings. This can be very dangerous on the road and it will increase your stopping distance.

To find a manufacturer's website you can use the NTTA website at www.ntta.co.uk and click onto 'Buyers Guide – Trailer Parts'. When consulting a manufacturer's site you will have to give them the following information:

- The width of the axle mounting points.
- The width of the trailer chassis, and
- Whether the design for the trailer platform or floor is to be positioned between the wheels or goes over the top of them as this determines the axle mounting points.

The decision on the chassis design will lead you to the correct choice of tyre size. If the platform or floor is to go over the wheels then you will

need the smallest tyre diameter that is able to carry the load of a fully laden trailer. The need for much smaller wheels is to enable the centre of gravity of the trailer to be as low as possible for safe towing as well as to obtain the correct coupling height from the ground. The trailer coupling height has to be between 395mm and 465mm to the centre of the towball location in the coupling head with the trailer level and laden. Depending on the GVW you may need to have more axles like the trailer shown above.

To determine the tyre size needed for a single axle trailer divide the GVW by two and look up the load index from the following chart to see which tyre just gives you a load figure in excess of that needed. For example if the trailer is to have a GVW of 1100kg then you will need a minimum load index of 99, giving you 1,120kg.

All tyres are speed rated and the following table gives the maximum speeds for each code letter. For your information the higher speed ratings of car tyres are included here.

J = 62mph (100km/h)
K = 68mph (110km/h)
L = 75mph (120km/h)
M = 81mph (130km/h)
N = 88mph (140km/h)
P = 94mph (150km/h)
Q = 100mph (160km/h)
R = 105mph (170km/h)
S = 113mph (180km/h)
T = 118mph (190km/h)
U = 124 mph (200km/h)
H = 130 mph (210km/h)
V = 149 mph (240km/h)
W = 168 mph (270km/h)
Y = 186 mph (300km/h)

You can buy axles where the suspension drop arm angle is different in order to suit

LOAD INDEX TABLE

Load Index	Kg	Load Index	Kg	Load Index	Kg	Load Index	Kg
60	250	71	345	82	475	93	650
61	257	72	355	83	487	94	670
62	265	73	365	84	500	95	690
63	272	74	375	85	515	96	710
64	280	75	387	86	530	97	730
65	290	76	400	87	545	98	750
66	300	77	412	88	560	99	775
67	307	78	425	89	580	100	800
68	315	79	437	90	600	101	825
69	325	80	450	91	615	102	850
70	335	81	462	92	630	103	875

underfloor axles as opposed to axles with the wheels outside the chassis. This allows full articulation of the suspension without fouling the bodywork of the trailer.

You should also consider whether you have any need to stand on the mudguards when loading a trailer or securing a load. If so, then you will need strong metal ones and might consider putting chequer plate on them, as shown below, to give a good surface on which to stand.

If you are having ramps you will need propstands to support the rear of the trailer when loading a vehicle or machines.

Regarding chassis design, if the trailer is a short one you could use the 'T' type design but if the trailer is a long one then it is better to go for an 'A' frame type. This gives greater lateral rigidity and torsional stiffness i.e. its resistance to flexing across the chassis frame. If you cannot calculate what sizes and types of steel sections to use, have a look at those used by trailer manufacturers. For instance, check trailers of a similar GVW to your preferred design at the trailer centre where you are buying the parts.

Building from a kit

This is the easiest way to build a small luggage type of trailer. These are supplied in flat pack form and are available from Halfords and most trailer centres. The components are quite simple to assemble as long as you follow the instructions carefully and do not try to do everything in a hurry. Here is a typical assembly operation, in this case for an Erde 122 trailer:

First, unpack the boxes. There are usually two of these with one containing the axle assembly. Lay out all the parts and check them against the contents list carefully and identify all the items. If anything is missing notify your supplier immediately to obtain the item as soon as possible.

It is best to work on a large table or a pair of trestles with an old door or a piece of board placed on top. The trailer is built upside down by

first taking the trailer base panel and placing it on the table with the underside facing upwards. The front end of the base panel has the drawbar tube/body tilt bracket mounting point.

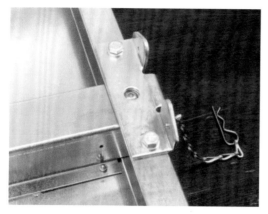

Fit this bracket using the two M8x20 set screws and then fit the axle unit making sure the suspension drop arms, carrying the hubs, face to the rear of the trailer base panel. Do not fully tighten any of the bolts at this time.

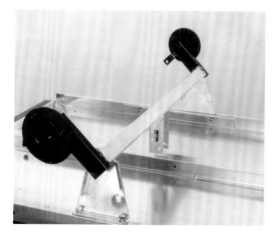

Now fit the drawbar tube making sure that the coupling is facing the floor with the skid

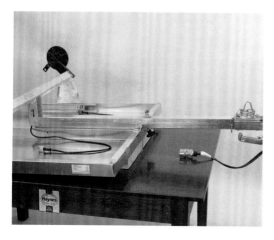

plate facing upwards. The end of the tube is fastened into the locating bracket in the centre of the axle using the M10x70 bolt.

Next, attach the drawbar tube guide to the upper side and screw on the plastic handle checking that the hook goes over the drawbar guide.

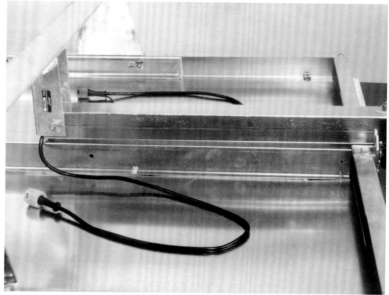

The rear lighting unit is fitted next by slotting it into the bottom panel with the two holes at the top. This unit is then fastened to the central reinforcing support member using the M8x16 dome head set screw.

Unroll the electrical cable and clip it to the central support member and connect the yellow plug into the socket on the yellow side of the rear light unit followed by the green plug in the green side socket. The plug has a lug so it can only be fitted in alignment with the corresponding cut-out on the socket.

Fully tighten all the nuts and bolts with the exception of the mudguard bolts and then turn the trailer over on to its wheels.

The trailer bodywork can now be fixed in place starting with the side panels with two M8x20 set screws per side, but do not fully tighten the fasteners yet. Slide the end panel on to the rear hinges and then secure it to the side panels with the two snap latches. This leaves the front panel to be fixed from the front and

The mudguards can now be fitted loosely using the slots, then adjusted and tightened later when the wheels and side panels are fitted.

The wheels can now be fitted, with the tyre inflation valve facing outwards of course. The wheel nuts have a domed end and a flat end and the domed end needs to be in contact with the wheel surface so that the wheel self centres on the hub when they are tightened.

underneath with six M8x20 set screws. At this point the rear triangular reflectors and fog lamp supports can be fitted. These first slot into the side panels and then into the bottom of the rear light unit using four M8x20 and four M6x10 screws. Now connect the rear fog light using the black cable coming from the rear of the green connector. This completes the assembly of the trailer and you can now tighten all the rear screws plus the mudguard screws.

Finally, double-check that all screws are tight and the tipping handle is located correctly on to the drawbar guide. In addition see that the safety 'R' clip is inserted into the screw thread showing through the top of the black tipping release knob. This can be seen just in front of the trailer body on the main drawbar.

Your trailer is now ready for use, but for easier manoeuvring you could fit a jockey wheel to the drawbar. A range of extras is available for these trailers including a spare wheel carrier and a locking hard-top cover made from ABS plastic.

These trailers are very light in weight and when towing without a load you must take care when passing over road humps as they can bounce around. Trailer suspension characteristics are such that they operate much better when loaded but you can have hydraulic dampers fitted which make a big improvement to the ride and towing stability.

Note: After the first 25 miles of towing you should stop and check the tightness of the wheel nuts.

PREPARING YOUR VEHICLE FOR TOWING

A few years ago you could simply bolt a towbar to the back of the car, tap into the car's electrics and away you would go.

Not anymore, as the electrics on modern cars and light commercials have changed so much and now have multiplex CAN bus wiring, bulb failure warning devices and even computerised anti-snake braking programmes. Making a wrong connection could be a very expensive mistake indeed.

Info

WHAT IS CAN?

This stands for Controller Area Network. This system, developed by Robert Bosch GmbH, sends information around a vehicle simultaneously in the form of timed signals. Each electrical unit on the vehicle has a different signal time and will only operate when a signal with the exact time is received.

A car requires preparation for towing, and depending on the make, model and specification, the amount of work needed can vary considerably. Owners who have good DIY or technical skills can carry out most of the work involved in fitting a towbar but unless using a car manufacturer's simple plug-in wiring kit (see the Vauxhall kit later in this chapter) it would be better to use a professional auto electrician.

As well as fitting a towbar and the towing electrics, there are other things that you can do to your vehicle to improve its overall towing ability, as shown below.

Engine performance improvements

You may feel your car could do with a little more power or torque to pull your trailer comfortably when fully laden. If so, you can now create more power by mechanical or electronic tuning. Emissions control regulations came into being in 1993 and have progressively been tightened since then. This has introduced the use of computer systems controlling the fuel supply for both petrol and diesel engines (and ignition on petrol engines) and the settings of these are usually conservative, to account for differing qualities of fuel. So there is some scope for improvement with the fuels available in Europe. The biggest demand for these performance upgrades nowadays is for turbo diesel engines as the improvement in power and more importantly torque can be quite considerable, and can prove very worthwhile when towing trailers up to the vehicle's maximum towing limit.

A surprising benefit for many cars is the improvement in fuel consumption after having the ECU's microprocessor 'chipped', the common name for a microprocessor being a 'chip'. Some motor manufacturers are starting to offer these performance add-ons, MG Rover for example, provided one for their diesel-powered 75 model, lifting the power from 116bhp to 131bhp and torque from 192lb ft to 221lb ft.

Powerklick electronic tuning kit from Diesel Tuning UK.

WHAT IS TORQUE?

This is the twisting force on the engine's crankshaft which turns the wheels and propels the car. The driver feels this as the force making the car accelerate. It is not the power of the engine doing this, it is the torque. There is a formula that lets you calculate the torque and it is:

$$\text{Torque} = \frac{\text{Power} \times 5252}{\text{Revs per Minute}}$$

Where units are Imperial e.g. torque in lb ft and power in bhp.

Turbo diesels produce higher torque at lower engine revolutions than petrol versions e.g. VW 1.4 petrol produces 75bhp and 93lb ft of torque whereas the VW 1.4 diesel also produces 75bhp but 144lb ft of torque. The difference is that the petrol engine needs to run at 4,235rpm but the diesel only 2,735rpm. They require different gear ratios to give comparable performance with petrol being the lowest geared.

If you think of a bicycle and you push the pedal down at 100lb force and the distance from the pedal to the centre of the chain wheel is 1 foot then the torque that you are producing is 100lb ft.

What if your turbo diesel does not have electronic control? You can still have some tuning carried out by altering the fuel supply by adjusting the setting on the fuel pump, allied to changing the pressure setting of the wastegate on the turbocharger itself. All turbochargers have a wastegate, which allows excess air pressure created by the turbocharger to be released, keeping the supply pressure within its pre-set limits. There is always a safety factor in the design of engines and the setting of the wastegate can be slightly increased without risk of engine damage. The companies that do this adjustment always give a guarantee covering you in case any damage should occur.

These modifications would require you to notify your insurance company and it may be found that an extra premium has to be paid. The supplier of the tuning kit should be able to give you the name of an insurance company that can provide you with cover for the vehicle after such modifications have been carried out.

Automatic gearboxes

A manual gearbox was the normal choice some time ago for towing, as automatic gearboxes had a poor reputation because of problems experienced with overheating of gearbox oils causing failure of the gearbox. Modern automatic gearboxes are far superior with improved means of gear changing. The most conventional ones still use a torque converter to enable setting off without a clutch which allows some degree of slip in lower gears, but the use

of a lock-up mechanism is now standard on higher gears giving improved performance and better fuel consumption. The control of gearboxes is now electronic with yet another onboard ECU providing the management of the gearchange points and allowing sequential manual gear changing.

The temperature of gearbox oil is still very important and most automatic transmissions use external oil coolers, usually built into the bottom of the car's water-cooling radiator. If you are unsure if your automatic has an external oil cooler have a look underneath the car and see if there are two hydraulic hoses coming from the gearbox. Follow these to see if one goes to one side of the car's radiator and if the other appears on the other side. If so, you have a gearbox oil cooler, but is it an efficient one?

Some gearbox coolers are simply a pipe of around 12–15mm in diameter, which passes through the bottom of the engine's radiator from one side to the other. This does not have a great cooling effect, as it is only the oil in immediate contact with the walls of the pipe that receives any cooling effect from the air passing through the radiator. Good coolers have the same appearance and construction as the radiator i.e. they have a number of narrow tubes through which the oil flows. These narrow tubes provide a larger surface area for the oil to benefit from the airflow through the cooler giving a cooling effect up to 50 times greater than the simple round pipe through the bottom of the radiator. You can check with your car manufacturer to see what type is fitted and whether an auxiliary oil cooler would be required. A complete kit is available for

Kenlowe oil cooler on Vauxhall Signum .

Front view.

Side view.

Top view.

Towing mirrors

You are required to see down both sides of the trailer that you are towing. If you cannot do this with the existing door mirrors you must fit extension mirrors. Some cars have very heavily styled shapes and universal designs of mirrors may not fit, but your car manufacturer will have some purpose-made versions. These will be available from your local franchised dealer. Note that mirrors must not protrude more than 800mm beyond the width of your trailer.

Suspension aids

If your car has soft rear suspension or a long overhang you may require the rear suspension to be 'beefed up' by fitting some form of spring assisters. Overhang is the distance from the centre of the rear wheels to the back of the car. Cars with the longest overhang are typically estate cars or saloons and those with the shortest are usually hatchbacks. As far as the suspension is concerned the ones that are best for towing are those with the shortest overhang as the nose weight has less effect and reduces pitching movement.

Pitching is the vertical up and down movement applied to the towball by the trailer when towing. On cars with soft rear suspension pitching can be annoying and may cause passengers to suffer from travel sickness. Some cars have self-levelling rear suspension as standard, or as an optional extra, being more commonly found as standard on estate cars e.g. the Ford Mondeo Estate, as they are built to carry heavier loads than saloon or hatchback versions. Large Citroën cars have the hydractive self-levelling suspension as standard and are looked upon as good towcars. The author has had extensive use of these cars finding the suspension to be really good with greatly reduced pitching.

Spring assisters can significantly reduce sag and pitching by stiffening up the suspension when towing. Assisters come in a number of forms such as rubber inserts into the spring coils, additional smaller coil springs either positioned inside or adjacent to the existing springs, or by replacing the rear shock absorbers for ones that can be inflated by compressed air. The latter can either be inflated by an external airline or by an onboard air compressor, or ones like the Boge Nivomat type which self-level themselves when driven over bumps in the road. Don't forget that for stable towing the 'A' frame/drawbar of the

around £110 whereas a replacement gearbox or rebuild could be over £1,000, so it is a relatively small sum for peace of mind.

It is far more relaxing towing with an automatic gearbox especially when starting on an incline, in stop-and-start traffic conditions and when reversing. However if you are towing in hilly or mountainous districts with a heavily laden trailer or caravan it would be very wise to have an auxiliary gearbox oil cooler fitted. We are fortunate in this country to have a specialist manufacturer of such auxiliary gearbox oil coolers, Kenlowe, which supplies models to fit most cars. The following photographs show the Kenlowe auxiliary gearbox oil cooler fitted to a Vauxhall Signum 3.0 V6 CDTI car before the bumper is refitted.

Far left: Monroe ride-leveller air-assisted damper.

Left: Grayston rubber inserts.

Selection of spring assisters from Grayston.

Below: Typical installation of helper spring.

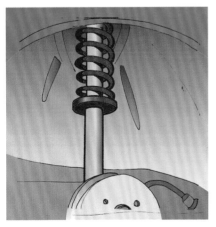

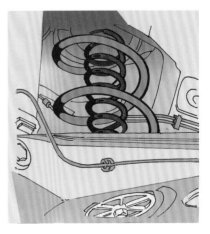

trailer should be parallel with the ground or facing slightly nose down when the trailer is attached to the car and laden. It must never point nose up to the towing vehicle.

Stabilisers

If you intend to use a stabiliser when towing, the type that you need to use requires careful choice of the design of towbar to take into account the fittings needed for the stabiliser. The towbars that are the simplest to use with a stabiliser are the traditional ones with a bolt on towball (known as a flanged ball or ball and bracket – see page 73) using two bolts. The attachment bracket for blade type stabilisers is clamped between the towball flange and the towbar. If you choose a swan neck towbar you will need a clamp on adapter to fit the blade-type stabiliser. Be careful here as most swan neck designs have a tapered cross-section reducing along its length to the underside of the towball. If there is no parallel section at the towbar end a clamp may not grip properly. (See later section on towbar choice.)

Nearly all stabilisers work by introducing

> ## Tip
>
> **DON'T FORGET**
> Fitting a stabiliser will not correct a badly set up outfit. It is a safety aid for well set up outfits.

friction into the system in order to reduce the speed of any turning motion.

The most common design of stabiliser seen today is the friction-head type particularly on caravans, but which is not so common on trailers. This is mainly because most trailers do not have high bodywork and suffer less from the effects of side winds or the forces produced by large goods vehicles when overtaking a trailer. This design has a larger coupling head which contain pads made out of a friction material and these are clamped around the towball when connected to the car. They operate in a similar way to brake pads by restricting the turning motion – in other words slowing down the movement of the trailer relative to the towball. There are three makers of this type of stabiliser, AL-KO Kober, Winterhoff and Westfalia.

The original AL-KO AKS 1300 stabiliser has two friction pads situated one on each side of the towball. This position damps out a side-to-side swaying motion but did little as regards pitching. They revised the design for the AKS 2004 model to include four pads. The extra two being positioned to the front and rear of the towball to damp out pitching motion.

Care must be taken when fitting this design of stabiliser to a towbar that has a flanged towball, as there may not be enough clearance

for the coupling head. You must fit the towball with the extended neck made by AL-KO to avoid any possible damage to the car bumper and to the neck of a standard towball. An AL-KO towball is supplied in the stabiliser kit but take care to ask for the correct towball from the vendor if buying a second-hand trailer or caravan that has the same make stabiliser already fitted. Their towball will have a type approval label on with AL-KO stamped on it. As they do not supply standard towballs this is your guarantee that it is the correct design for use with their AKS stabilisers. If you tow with a large 4x4 which has the spare wheel mounted on the rear door you may have a problem with the operating handle hitting the spare wheel before the handle is high enough to allow the coupling to connect to the towball. If this happens you can now buy a removable handle kit from AL-KO Kober.

Westfalia SSK stabiliser.

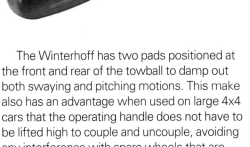

The Winterhoff has two pads positioned at the front and rear of the towball to damp out both swaying and pitching motions. This make also has an advantage when used on large 4x4 cars that the operating handle does not have to be lifted high to couple and uncouple, avoiding any interference with spare wheels that are hung on the back of the vehicle.

The Westfalia SSK has two pads positioned to the sides of the towball but differs from the above designs in having a gas strut as a means of keeping constant pressure on the ball.

The Westfalia and Winterhoff do not require a change of flanged towball as their head design leaves sufficient clearance from the bumper and the underside of the towball.

There are some precautions to take when using friction-head stabilisers. They are designed to operate dry so please make sure that your towball is degreased before hitching

up. If there is any paint or plated finish to the towball remove this with the use of emery cloth so that the pads act directly onto a clean metal surface. When manoeuvring at low speed it is best to release the clamping force on the ball, to avoid excess stress on the towball, by lifting or partially lifting the clamp handle. There are trailer weight limitations with friction-head stabilisers as they only go up to 2,700kg GVW.

Apart from the need to use AL-KO's towball for flange-mounted applications there are no other brackets or locating lugs on the towbar. The older friction disc type of stabiliser does require a mounting bracket to be fitted to the towbar.

Far left: Winterhoff WS 3000 stabiliser.

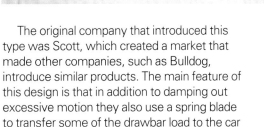

The original company that introduced this type was Scott, which created a market that made other companies, such as Bulldog, introduce similar products. The main feature of this design is that in addition to damping out excessive motion they also use a spring blade to transfer some of the drawbar load to the car

Bulldog 2000 stabiliser.

helping to reduce pitching. The spring blade is located in a bracket attached to one side of the trailer drawbar. For larger trailers with a higher gross vehicle weight you can have this type of stabiliser in twin format fitted to both sides of the drawbar.

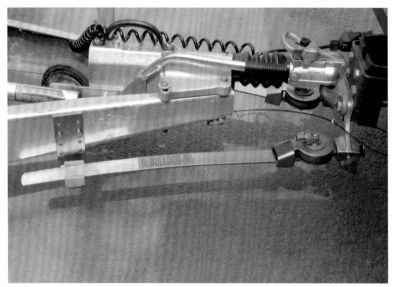

Above: Bulldog 400 twin stabiliser.

Above right: Straightliner stabiliser.

There can be a problem in fitting blade-type stabilisers to cars with swan neck towbars. With the normal British style towbar with the flanged ball bolted on with two bolts it is simple to fit the stabiliser bracket in between the towbar mounting flange and the towball, but a swan neck does not have this facility. You can buy a mounting clamp that is fitted around the neck but if there is insufficient parallel length on the neck before it starts to taper up to the ball the bracket will not hold tight and will rotate around the bracket. For swan neck towbars it is much better to use the friction-head type of stabiliser.

Tip

DON'T FORGET
If you fit a stabiliser bracket behind the towball you will need longer towball bolts. There must be at least two clear threads showing through the nuts when tight.

An interesting stabiliser without the use of friction material is the Straightliner introduced by the makers of the Rollsafe Trapezium stabiliser (see later in this section). This has a vee shaped section and if the trailer swings too much there is a gas strut that physically resists this movement and pushes the trailer back into line with the towing vehicle using the vee section as a self centring device.

The most effective type of stabilisers, however, did not have friction materials incorporated in them. A twin blade system from Vasseur, a French company, had the blades pivoting in Oilite bushes, hence no friction to speak of, relying on the spring pressure of the blades to self centre the trailer. This worked very well and was ideal for trailers up to 3,500kg.

There was an excellent design from South Africa called the Rollsafe Trapezium. This had the towball mounted on swing links attached to the towbar and worked by effectively transferring the rotational pivot point (the towball) to a position further forward under the car usually around the rear axle centre line.

This created a virtual pivot point that made the trailer behave more like an articulated trailer than a drawbar trailer. In effect this increased the distance of the trailer axle from the towball. The greater that distance the more stable will be the trailer. The disadvantage was the 'trailer cut in' when cornering was increased and it was easy to clip the kerb. Experience soon overcame that problem. Why aren't these available today? The problem is that they could not be approved to the European Directive 94/20/EC, which came into force on 1 August 1998. This directive states that only type-approved towbars could be fitted to all European Whole Vehicle type-approved vehicles first registered from that date. It can, of course still be used on vehicles registered before that date. So a superb product was removed from the market due to the way the directive was worded.

Towbar choice

You have a wide choice of towbar types today and the decisions you make regarding any other uses of the towbar can have an influence in the actual design and manufacturer of the towbar. Are you fitting a stabiliser and if so what type? Are you fitting a cycle carrier?

If you are using a Scott-type blade stabiliser or fitting a cycle carrier you are best advised to use a traditional British-style flanged ball towbar as the attachment point because the stabiliser or cycle carrier can be mounted between the towball and the towbar face. If you used a swan neck towbar there is difficulty in fitting an attachment point that stays in place and does not twist around the neck when in use.

Towbars come in three designs known as fixed, removable or detachable. Fixed towbars are those meant to remain on the vehicle at all times ready for use and this description is usually applied to the flanged ball design.

A removable towbar is a swan neck design where the towball and neck can be removed by using tools so the towbar frame is not left sticking out from the back of the car. This is

ideal if you tow very little and do not want the towbar to be on sight for the rest of the time when not towing. This can be inconvenient to use and led to the introduction of the detachable design. A fixed towbar could be described as removable as you can simply unbolt the flanged towball but it still leaves the towbar sticking out and can be painful to anybody walking into it.

A removable ball swan neck design from ORIS.

A detachable towbar is a design where the swan neck ball complete with neck, can be very quickly taken off the towbar without using any tools. Some designs come with a key-operated lock as an anti-theft device to prevent your trailer being stolen while coupled up to your car.

Far left: Fixed Swan Neck Towbar from Bosal.

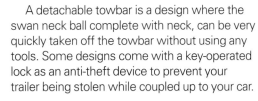

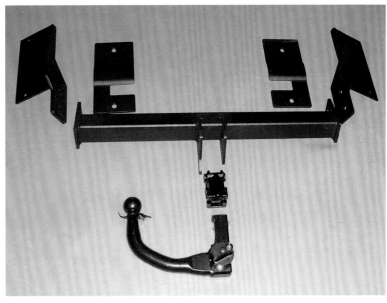

Other designs require the towball to be rotated through 90˚ or 180˚ in order to detach the towball, which is impossible to do if you have a trailer attached to it. The electrical sockets can be swung away as they are mounted on a swivelling bracket so when you are not towing there is nothing to see. This

A Witter Quantum detachable towbar.

design is more expensive than the flanged ball type but the extra cost may be worth it for the aesthetic aspect of the design.

Witter stowball detachable towbar.

The latest really up-market design is the powered swinging towbar where the towball is hidden under the car when not in use but is swung out by electric motors simply by pushing a button on the dashboard. Very nice but at a cost of £750 for the one fitted to a Porsche Cayenne.

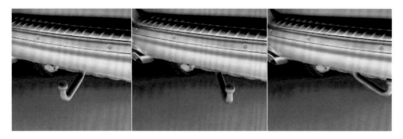

An interesting development has come from Witter Towbars who have developed a design of towbar that can be easily converted from a fixed type to a detachable in just a few minutes. You could have a detachable bar for towing and simply convert it back to a flange face for carrying cycles when not towing.

If your car was first registered after 1 August 1998 and you intend to fit a blade-type stabiliser

Witter flange ball towbar.

or a cycle carrier between the towball and the towbar face ensure that the make you are considering has a type-approval certificate that allows this. The European Directive does not allow any item to be fitted there unless the towbar has been tested with a spacer. Most towbar makers have had their products approved to allow for a 15mm thick item to be bolted between the towball and the towbar face plate but this may not be enough for your make of cycle carrier etc. Witter has now obtained approvals covering items up to 25mm thick.

When deciding on your choice of towbar check to see if there is a suitable mounting point for the breakaway cable. Ideally this should be in the form of a steel ring or slot through which you can pass the clip of the cable and fasten it back on itself.

This should really best be situated within 100mm of the towball centre but with detachable designs this is not possible and you may require a longer breakaway cable. Take care to ask the question about attachment points for the breakaway cable. Some towbars do not have one and all you can do is loop the cable around the towball which is permitted with flanged ball or swan neck towbars, but this practice is not recommended in the British Standard Code of Practice for detachable towbars.

One aspect of towbar choice that you may not have considered is whether the design requires a part of the rear bumper or skirt to be cut away. Many cars start off life as company-owned vehicles, quite often being leased from a finance company. Most finance companies require a towbar to be removed at the end of the lease period and if the cut out portion of the bumper is left exposed they would require a new replacement bumper to be fitted at a quite considerable cost. These days it is not unusual to pay in the order of £500 to cover the supply, painting and fitting of a new bumper. If you make the wrong choice you could be responsible for this cost whereas if you ask different towbar makers before having one fitted you may find one can be supplied which avoids the need for such cut outs.

Your car dealer may tell you that if you have a towbar supplied and fitted by anyone other than themselves that your car's warranty may be deemed to be null and void. This is not correct as all towbars made for cars first sold from 1 August 1998 must use a type-approved towbar that meets European Directive 94/20/EC. This means that any type-approved towbar will use all the car manufacturer's mounting points and meet relevant dimensions stated in the vehicle's European Whole Vehicle Type Approval Certificate. European Directive 95/48/EC requires this information to be printed in the owner's handbook supplied with a vehicle.

Recent changes in Block Exemption laws mean that a car manufacturer cannot insist that any replacement parts fitted to the car can only be supplied by the car maker. You can now use other makes of spare parts but they must be of a similar quality as the original. Towbars, of course, are of a similar quality, as they all have to be type tested to the 94/20/EC directive. Car manufacturers, in any case, do not make their own towbars; they simply develop them in conjunction with one of the many towbar makers and then sell them under their own brand name. What the car manufacturer will not

do is cover any other make of towbar under the car's warranty, but it will be covered by the towbar manufacturer's own warranty.

If you will be towing with a 3,500kg light commercial vehicle or a truck with a GVW exceeding 3,500kg up to 7500kg you may need to tow a trailer that has an eye coupling instead of a 50mm ball. You can have a combination ball and pin coupling fitted. This bolts onto the faceplate of the traditional two-bolt flanged towbar.

If you only tow with a commercial vehicle you can also fit a Shocklink between the towbar faceplate and the combination coupling/towball. This device has springs that allow the up and down loads exerted on the towball to be absorbed, thus reducing the severity of the load and preventing excess forces being applied to the trailer's drawbar.

Towbar electrics

The electrical connections needed to tow a trailer are to operate all the road lights on the trailer, so just a 12N socket is required. This provision is usually referred to as 'single electrics'. Twin electrics are needed when a caravan is towed and the extra wiring provides power to the caravan appliances and also for a reversing light as there is no spare wire on the 12N socket for this. A reversing light is not legally required on a trailer. This connection uses a 12S socket, which has a pin layout that is not

Dixon-Bate combination ball and pin coupling

Dixon-Bate shocklink coupling damper.

compatible with the 12N so you cannot connect with the wrong plug. There were changes made to the pin designations around 1998 and the wrong pin use can cause problems both on the car and the caravan. For full details you should consult *The Caravan Manual* by John Wickersham published by Haynes.

You have to be very careful these days when wiring your car up for trailer electrics as modern cars can have very sophisticated electronics on board and any damage caused through incorrect wiring can be a very expensive mistake to rectify. On older cars it was simple to tap into the car's lighting circuit usually at a rear light housing to provide the current for the trailer lights, but it is not that easy now. Around 1990 luxury cars began to be fitted with multiplexed CAN bus wiring (Controller Area Network). Use of this wiring system has been progressively fitted to lower priced cars since then and is now found on all cars either fully or in part.

It is the system of sending signals around the car that is known as CAN bussing and every electrical item fitted has a transmitter and a receiver. When, for instance, you apply the footbrake while driving, the transmitter for that operation sends a timed signal along the wiring and the receivers in the wiring listen out for signals. The time or length of the signals varies according to the device being asked to switch on so when the stoplight receiver records a signal of the correct length it switches on the stoplights. The driver is not aware of this happening as the signal time is in milliseconds so it appears to be instantaneous.

It can also handle problems in the system. If, for instance, a stop lamp bulb has blown the processor controlling the CAN bus system may change the signal direction to use the adjacent tail light bulb and illuminate it at the required 21 watts as all the bulbs are rated at 21W. This also operates in the reverse manner so if a tail light bulb has blown the CAN bus system can change over to using the stoplight bulb and illuminates it at 5 watts. The wiring carries all the signals at a very low current (10mA) for every electrical item fitted through the same wire at the same time, known as Data Share, with each item having a different signal length.

This reduces the normal wiring loom used on a car to a two-wire system, saving considerable weight and complexity, but can create problems when you want to tap into the wiring to connect up a trailer socket. If you inadvertently make a connection in the wiring before a receiver you can cause serious problems with the operation of all the car's electronics so you must be careful when looking at the electrical components fitted to your car.

How do you know if your car has multiplexed CAN bus wiring? You could always ask your car dealer's service department, but a typical give away is if your car has features that were not found on cars made a few years ago. Does your car's interior light fade away after you have shut the door instead of turning off immediately? Do the headlights remain on for a short while when you have parked your car at night allowing you to see where you are walking up to your front door? Features like these will indicate that your car has multiplex wiring.

Towbar fitters used to tap directly into the rear light wires to obtain the feeds for the trailer wiring but bulb failure warning devices and the need to cut out rear fog and reversing lights brought about the introduction of by-pass relays. Nowadays, fitters normally take a power supply straight from the car's battery for the trailer lighting and just use a relay for the signal for each light's function. A relay is a switch, using an electromagnetic coil or solid state electronics which takes the signal at a low current from the car light and turns the equivalent trailer light on using the power straight from the battery. This can cause problems where the car manufacturer has used the anti-lock brake system (ABS) sensors to do other jobs such as traction control (TCS), electronic skid prevention (EPS), and even anti-snaking systems.

This system, like others, started life on expensive 4x4 vehicles but is now available on the new Vauxhall Astra as part of the £350 Towing Pack, which includes automatic load levelling, hill start assist (HSA) which stops the vehicle rolling back on hills, and the innovative trailer stability programme (TSP). This latter programme senses when a trailer is swaying by using yaw sensors and reacts by taking over the car's braking system and accelerator pedal (throttle) control and applies or releases them in a programmed sequence to pull the swaying trailer into line. The driver does not have to do anything other than keep the steering in a straight line. With the car maker's own wiring kit the system senses when the trailer's electrical plug is connected and knows that there is a trailer hitched up to the car. This, therefore, brings the anti-snake programme into play should it be required.

Obviously, if a towbar fitting company uses traditional bypass relays this system may not operate as required and they could find that they may be held liable should an accident occur while towing and serious injury or a fatality is the end result.

The safe way to ensure that all of the car's on-board systems work as designed is to use the car manufacturer's own trailer wiring system kit. Some towbar manufacturers are starting to supply aftermarket wiring kits containing a microprocessor that can integrate with the car's on-board computers to control the operations correctly. These are also becoming available from specialist wiring kit suppliers e.g. Right Connections (UK) Ltd.

The current Vauxhall Signum/Vectra original equipment manufacturer's (OEM) wiring kit is shown below. The 'black box' with the male connector built in is the electronic control unit (ECU) containing the microprocessor chip. It is extremely easy to use this type of wiring kit, as you do not have to make any connections directly into any wires. The ECU simply plugs in to a socket adjacent to the fuses in the rear boot space. You will have to take the car to a Vauxhall dealer later to have some additional software downloads written onto the microprocessor to enable some functions to operate such as to enable the car's rear fog lamp to be switched off when the trailer is connected and for the graphic instrument display (if fitted in the centre of the dashboard) to be activated. The cable unit is again simply plugged into a

socket connector (next to the ECU socket) in the fuse box and fed through the spare wheel well and out to the seven-pin socket. The cable needs to be earthed using the white wire which has a round terminal. This cable also includes a ready-prepared red wire for the power supply to the 12S caravan electrics, if being fitted at the same time.

SEVEN-PIN AND 13-PIN SOCKETS
If you buy a single-electric wiring kit you will receive either a normal seven-pin 12N socket, or more commonly now in OEM-supplied wiring kits, a German type 13-pin socket as shown from Hella. The 13-pin socket may only have seven pins in it and is not compatible with the pin layout in a seven-pin plug. You would have to buy twin electrics to get the full 13 pins installed, but check as not all actually have all 13 pins fitted. Some, for example, are only fitted with ten pins. This is the car industry's way of cutting pennies off the cost of a component. The problem is that for UK caravan wiring you need one of the missing pins and you must go back to your car dealer and demand a socket with a full complement of pins.

The next problem with 13-pin sockets is that there are three designs all with different pin layouts. Those supplied with European car maker's wiring kits are usually to the German pin layout. The size and layout of the pins is unique. The Benelux countries prefer a 13-pin system called WeSt Multicon where the pin layout has the standard 12N layout of seven pins in the centre of the socket and the extra 6 round pins set out in a circle around the edge of the socket as shown right. This has the advantage that you can tow any trailer without changing the normal seven-pin plug on the trailer.

The third design also has the standard 12N seven-pin format in the centre but has six flat pins around the edge and is commonly found in France.

You can see from the above that the more complicated the wiring the more careful you need to be if you decide to wire up your car yourself. Unless you are experienced in car wiring it is better to use a professional towbar fitter, particularly one that has been trained by the National Trailer and Towing Association (NTTA). If you do want to fit your own towbar then the following chapter shows a typical installation with a bumper cut out. It also covers the use of by-pass relays to avoid problems with bulb failure warning devices and other features used on many of today's cars.

Hella 13-pin socket (Jaeger design pin layout) to BS EN ISO 11446

WeSt Multicon 13-pin plug and socket. Note the 12N pin layout in the centre.

FITTING A TOWBAR

You can fit a towbar yourself, or leave it to the experts – it's your choice. The towbar itself can often be an easy operation on many vehicles, but some have bumpers which are difficult to remove without damaging the mounting points.

It is the electrics where you can encounter problems. Twin-electric sockets are fitted in this installation, although a single 12N socket is suitable for most trailers because a supply is only required for the trailer lighting. If you are intending to tow a caravan you should have twin (12N +12S) electrics fitted at the same time, as it will be much cheaper than having the 12S fitted later. We are having a 12S system fitted to this car.

Among the most popular cars which have towbars fitted today are the Ford Mondeo and Vauxhall Vectra, although among the easiest models to equip are Land Rover Discoveries and Ford Transits.

A typical charge for fitting a flanged-ball towbar and single 12N electrics will be around £250 plus VAT, but it could be up to about £400. It depends on the vehicle, and it is not necessarily related to the initial cost of the car — the less popular makes of car means smaller production batches of the towbar and hence higher costs. The complexity of fitting can increase the actual time involved resulting in higher labour costs. Bumper removal or the need for a cutaway in the bumper are examples of this.

If you decide on a detachable towbar you will find that you will have to allow an extra £100–160 over the price of a fixed bar.

You should also remember to take into account that a towbar adds some 10–15kg to the kerb weight of the car and this has to be taken into account in your load calculations.

Tip

WHAT TYPE OF TOWBALL SHOULD I HAVE?
A flanged ball enables you to easily fit the blade-type stabiliser socket or a cycle carrier. It is difficult, or impossible to do this, with swan neck or detachable types.

1 The car used for this towbar fitting is a Subaru Legacy Outback, 1999 model. As a point of interest it's often easier to fit towbars to an estate car than to a saloon – the flat loading area at the rear is easier to work with. In general, three-door hatchbacks are the most difficult to fit.

As this car was first registered after 1 August 1998, the towbar has to be type approved to European Directive 94/20/EC. As a result of type approval, many companies are now happier to allow the fitting of towing brackets to their fleet vehicles, as long as bumper cut outs are not made. For cars registered before this date, the towbar does not have to carry type approval.

The use of hydraulic ramps, as shown here, is a real boon to towbar fitting because of the number of times the car has to go up and down.

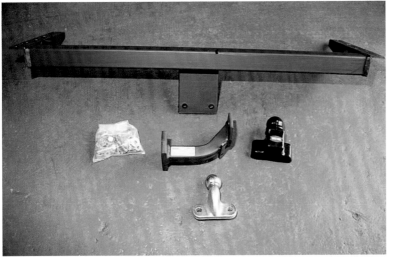

2 Here is a typical towing bracket and towball, supplied in this instance by Witter Towbars. All towing brackets are prone to rust, although this bar has an oven-baked primer finish, which is corrosion proof in its own right, or they can be finished with proprietary rust inhibitor finishes such as Waxoyl or Hammerite. Please do not paint over the type approval label as this must be legible at all times.

3 This is the type approval label. It shows the manufacturer's name, the part number, country where the towbar was approved (e11 = UK), maximum permitted nose weight (S value), and the approval number issued by the testing authority (in this case, the UK Vehicle Certification Agency).

Prior to type approval in 1998, there was little in the way of legislation regarding the design and manufacture of towbars.

4 Instructions are included with each towbar. Here, it is all on just one side of an A4 sheet. Also included is a detailed, three dimensional diagram.

5 Removing the interior trim is the first step. Not only does this make the working environment easier, it also prevents the likelihood of any of the trim being accidentally damaged during the fitting. The trim is put aside, on a protective surface for safety.

Here, the trim comes out easily and, later, is similarly straightforward to refit.

The boot area is now clear. A lot of cars have false floors in their boots.

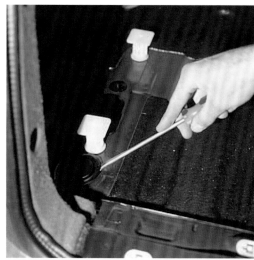

6 All the trim has now been removed.

7 These rubber covers flip out to reveal bolts, which secure the bumper.

8 Moving the car up on the ramps means the fitter can check underneath for additional bolts holding the bumper, which are then removed. At qualified fitting centres such as this, air tools are available for this work.

9 As mentioned in the towbar fitting instructions, there are a couple of bolts just inside the wheel arches.

10 Typical of many modern cars, the Subaru has a considerable plastic bumper moulding. Sometimes such items are attached by plastic studs, which can break when they are forced.

11 Inside the luggage area there is another retainer for the bumper moulding.

12 The bumper moulding is now ready to be lifted off. In cases like this, it is sometimes advisable to employ a second pair of hands – it helps prevent the possibility of damage if one end is accidentally dropped, or if the moulding 'flips' when it becomes loose from the bodywork.

13 With the bumper surround off you can see the slot for the towing bracket, just above the exhaust tailpipe.

14 The brackets from inside the bumper surround can now be removed and the bumper placed on a padded surface to eliminate any danger of scratching. This Subaru's bumper is made in two pieces but on older cars, the bumper could have more sections.

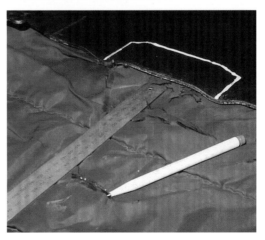

15 A section of the original bumper moulding, highlighted here – now needs to be removed for the towing bracket.

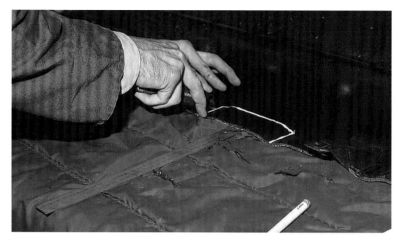

16 A sharp knife is used for this, rather than a saw which could leave a burred edge. Sometimes a cutting mark is provided by the vehicle manufacturer, but not in this case.

17 Some of the original bumper brackets need to be retained. Here, the fitter drills out the spot welds.

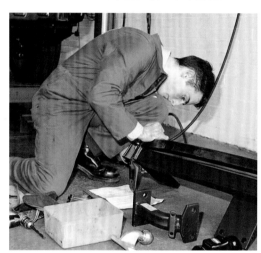

18 The original bumper bracket is attached to the towbar bracket . . .

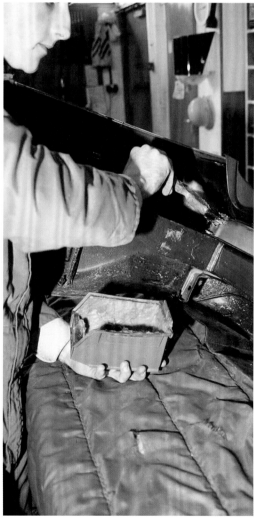

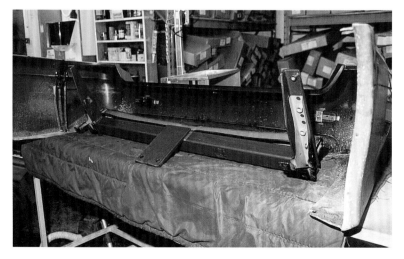

19 . . . and this piece then re-attached to the plastic bumper surround.

20 All metalwork is then treated with a rust inhibitor such as Waxoyl or a similar product.

21 Lifting the whole bumper and towing bracket section is again an easier job when there's a bit of additional help.

22 A quick check underneath reveals all is well . . .

23 . . . and the towing bracket can now be bolted into place. New bolts are supplied as part of the towbar package.

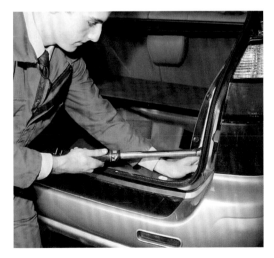

24 A torque wrench ensures all bolts are tightened to their recommended settings.

25 All the towing bracket mounting bolts tightened by this fitter are dabbed with a 'blob' of red paint. Not only is this the fitter's way of checking that he's tightened each bolt, it is also a useful future reference for the vehicle's owner.

26 The next stage is to bolt on this extension bracket with a plate to which the towball will be attached.

27 The final steps of the towbar fitting are to add the towball and the electric sockets. Again, any bolts here are daubed with paint as proof of correct tightening.

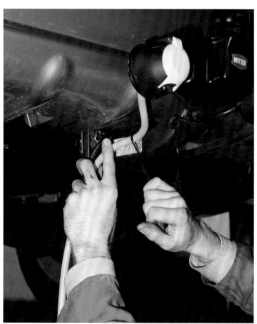

28 Finally, it is electrics. This is the plug of Subaru's OE wiring kit. Like many other motor manufacturers their latest models, have a plug already fitted for towbar electrics. If the wiring loom is only at the front of the vehicle, you may have to run wires through to it.

29 The wires from the 12S and 12N sockets are cable-clipped where possible, ready for threading back to the car's wiring loom.

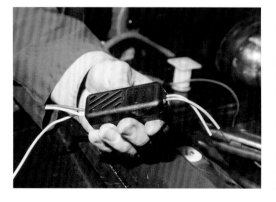

30 Now, here's a choice. Current legislation says you must have either an audible or a visual warning device to tell you that the trailer's direction indicator lights are working correctly when you're towing. We've opted here for a buzzer. Not only is it easier to fit, without the problem of having to run a wire to a light fitting near the dashboard and drilling a hole there, but they're also generally more reliable. Some makes of car have an extra 'tell-tale' in the instrument cluster usually in the form of a symbol of a caravan or a towbar.

31 Checking the feed from the plug on the wiring loom.

32 The earth wire must be fastened directly to the car's bodywork.

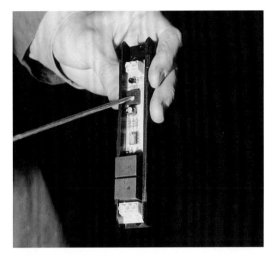

33 A self-switching relay is the next item to be fitted. This works on a voltage drop, to ensure the car battery isn't drained when the engine is turned off. This is for the power supply on a caravan if you have a 12S (twin electrics) as here. There's a screw adjustment for the voltage, depending on the age of the car and the condition of the battery.

34 A heavy duty power feed, using wire of at least 4mm² cross sectional area (csa) is now threaded direct from the battery to the rear of the Subaru, with the battery disconnected. If your car has a security-coded radio make sure you know the code number before disconnecting the battery. A fuse is fitted in-line, near the battery, then the wire is usually run through the engine bulkhead and on through the car, under trim, to the boot. Doing this throughout the car can sometimes be a problem, but this is not so here.

35 The final test, with this lights board, shows all is OK. A reversing light on a trailer is not a legal requirement.

36 Covers for the towball and electrics sockets aren't just there to look good – they offer protection from the elements when not towing and, in the case of the towball, prevent anyone accidentally smearing their clothing with grease.

Wiring diagrams for sockets and relays

SOCKET AND PLUG WIRING INSTRUCTION

12N Normal socket	*12S Supplementary socket (post 1998 caravans)*
1 Left turn indicator – yellow wire	1 Reverse light – yellow wire
2 Fog – blue wire	2 Spare – blue wire
3 Earth – white wire	3 Earth – white wire
4 Right turn indicator – green wire	4 Power feed and auxilliary battery charging – green wire
5 Right side light – brown wire	5 Spare – brown wire
6 Brake light – red wire	6 Fridge – red wire
7 Left side light and numberplate light – black wire	7 Earth for pin 6 – black wire

The terms 'right' and 'left' are when viewed from the rear of the vehicle.

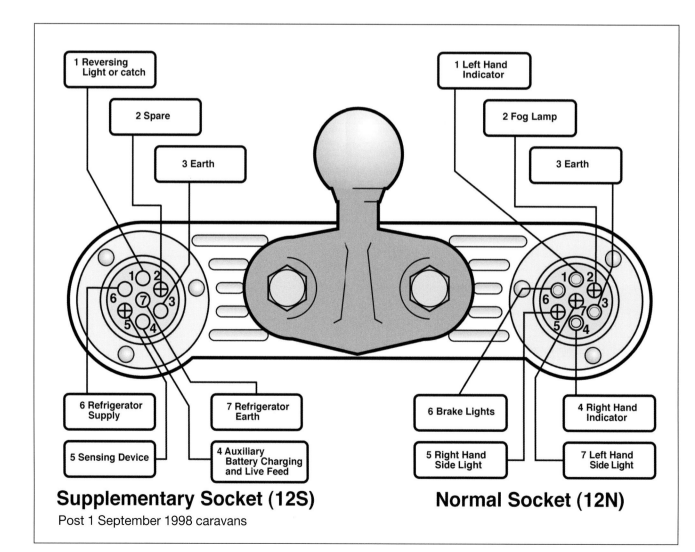

Supplementary Socket (12S)
Post 1 September 1998 caravans

Normal Socket (12N)

Depending on the age of the vehicle and the type of electrics, if you are not using the vehicle manufacturer's own wiring kit, relays will be required. The following diagrams show how to use these devices correctly. Please note that some cars may have wiring that differs from the colours shown so you must check each circuit to make sure that you are making the right connection.

On older manufactured seven-pin plugs and sockets, terminals were marked L, R, 31, 54, 54G, 58L and 58R. These are shown in the diagram below with their current markings.

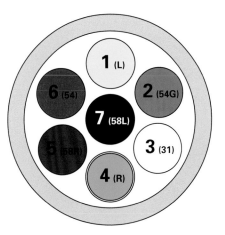

Pin No.	Function	12N Pin No.	12S Pin No.
1	Left hand indicator light	1	
2	Rear fog light	2	
3	Earth return for pins 1 to 8	3	
4	Right hand indicator light	4	
5	Right hand tail and marker lights	5	
6	Stop lights	6	
7	Left hand tail and marker lights	7	
8	Reversing light		1
9	Permanent power supply		4
10	Power supply to Fridge (ignition controlled)		6
11	Earth return for Fridge		7
12	Coding (if used) normally spare		2
13	Earth return for pin 9		3

13-PIN SOCKET (viewed from plug side)

Jaeger

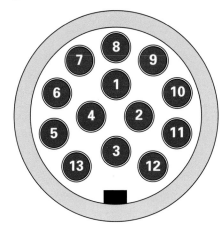

WeSt Multicon

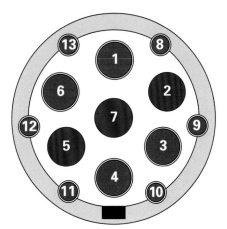

All the following
instructions are for
relays available from
Towbars & Trailers,
Chesterfield.

NB Colours may
vary between
manufacturers.
Instructions as listed
are a guideline only
and no responsibility
will be accepted for
incorrect
interpretation.

The word 'flasher'
denotes flashing
indicator lamp. '44str'
means 44 strands of
wire in the cable.

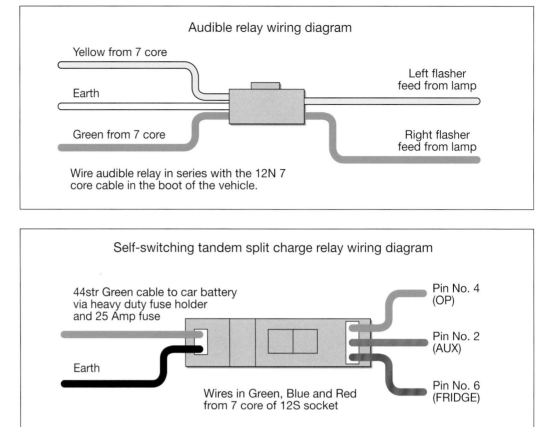

Audible relay wiring diagram

Yellow from 7 core

Earth

Green from 7 core

Left flasher
feed from lamp

Right flasher
feed from lamp

Wire audible relay in series with the 12N 7
core cable in the boot of the vehicle.

Self-switching tandem split charge relay wiring diagram

44str Green cable to car battery
via heavy duty fuse holder
and 25 Amp fuse

Earth

Pin No. 4
(OP)

Pin No. 2
(AUX)

Pin No. 6
(FRIDGE)

Wires in Green, Blue and Red
from 7 core of 12S socket

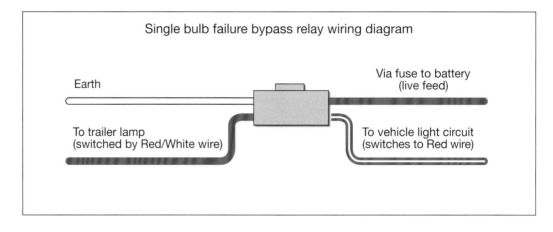

Single bulb failure bypass relay wiring diagram

Earth

Via fuse to battery
(live feed)

To trailer lamp
(switched by Red/White wire)

To vehicle light circuit
(switches to Red wire)

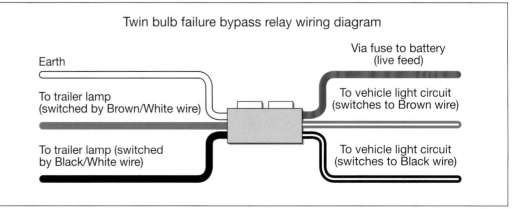

Twin bulb failure bypass relay wiring diagram

Via fuse to battery
(live feed)

Earth

To trailer lamp
(switched by Brown/White wire)

To vehicle light circuit
(switches to Brown wire)

To trailer lamp (switched
by Black/White wire)

To vehicle light circuit
(switches to Black wire)

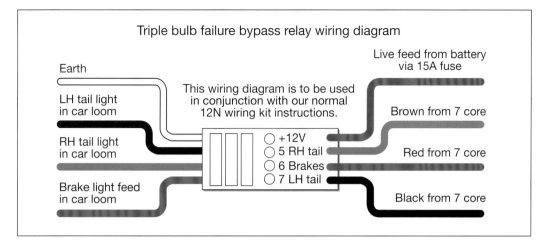

Triple bulb failure bypass relay wiring diagram

Earth

LH tail light in car loom

RH tail light in car loom

Brake light feed in car loom

This wiring diagram is to be used in conjunction with our normal 12N wiring kit instructions.

○ +12V
○ 5 RH tail
○ 6 Brakes
○ 7 LH tail

Live feed from battery via 15A fuse

Brown from 7 core

Red from 7 core

Black from 7 core

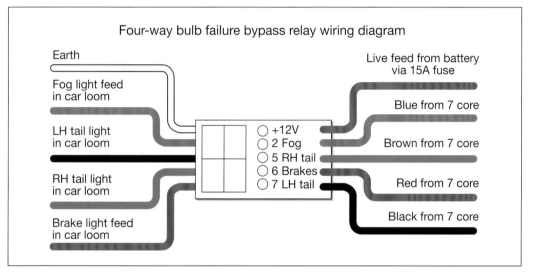

Four-way bulb failure bypass relay wiring diagram

Earth

Fog light feed in car loom

LH tail light in car loom

RH tail light in car loom

Brake light feed in car loom

○ +12V
○ 2 Fog
○ 5 RH tail
○ 6 Brakes
○ 7 LH tail

Live feed from battery via 15A fuse

Blue from 7 core

Brown from 7 core

Red from 7 core

Black from 7 core

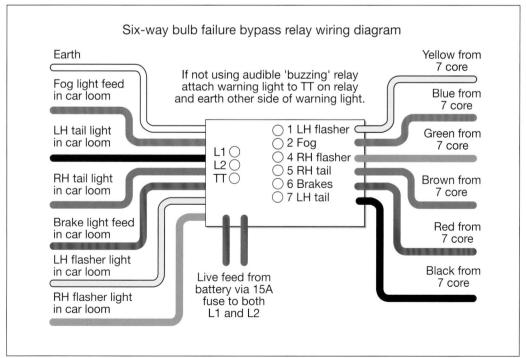

Six-way bulb failure bypass relay wiring diagram

Earth

Fog light feed in car loom

LH tail light in car loom

RH tail light in car loom

Brake light feed in car loom

LH flasher light in car loom

RH flasher light in car loom

If not using audible 'buzzing' relay attach warning light to TT on relay and earth other side of warning light.

L1 ○
L2 ○
TT ○

○ 1 LH flasher
○ 2 Fog
○ 4 RH flasher
○ 5 RH tail
○ 6 Brakes
○ 7 LH tail

Live feed from battery via 15A fuse to both L1 and L2

Yellow from 7 core

Blue from 7 core

Green from 7 core

Brown from 7 core

Red from 7 core

Black from 7 core

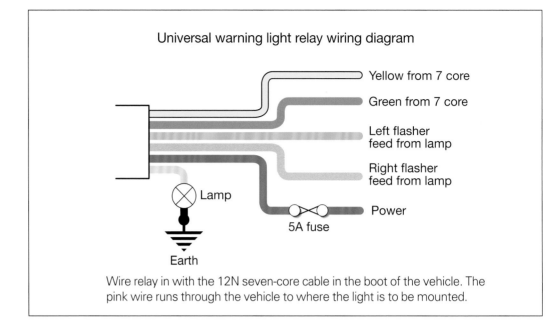

Universal warning light relay wiring diagram

Yellow from 7 core

Green from 7 core

Left flasher
feed from lamp

Right flasher
feed from lamp

Lamp

Power

5A fuse

Earth

Wire relay in with the 12N seven-core cable in the boot of the vehicle. The pink wire runs through the vehicle to where the light is to be mounted.

There is now a seven-way relay that contains the option for use on reversing lights with negative switches used on some vehicles.

The above wiring diagrams have been kindly supplied by Tony Maris of Towbars & Trailers, with all items available to the public from Davian Works, Storforth Lane, Chesterfield, Derbyshire S40 2TU. Telephone: 01246 202543; www.towitall.co.uk

If you are fitting a twin-electrics 12S or 13-pin system it may be worth having a modification to the wiring to ensure the caravan refrigerator works correctly while towing. Today's refrigerators can have heating elements of up to 225 watts requiring up to 18.75 amps at 12 volts with the added requirement of the caravan's leisure battery charging needs, all while towing. You may find that the refrigerator warning light flashes intermittently or the interior lights switch themselves off and on. You will also hear the voltage sensing relay fitted in the car cycling in and out. Added to this the main supplier of refrigerators to the caravan industry says that their products need over 11.5 volts to operate efficiently. You are most unlikely to achieve this voltage due to voltage drop through the sizes of wire used. The refrigerator makers say that if the length of the wire from the car battery to the refrigerator and back to the car's earthing point is less than 6m then wire with a cross sectional area (csa) of $6mm^2$

must be used and if it is more than 6m then wire of $10mm^2$ should be used. These sizes are not used or specified in the wiring standards used by either the car or caravan industry. Their standards call for wire with a csa of $2.5mm^2$ for the power supply. These industries must get together to modify the standards so that the current 12V power requirements for caravans can be accommodated without the need for additional wiring with heavier duty wire. You can use twin-feed and return wires as a substitution for single larger csa wires, as shown below.

What causes voltage drop?

Voltage drop may be caused by poor connections, undersize wire and/or through the circuit board of the relay itself. Given that, at best, we are starting with 14.2V at the vehicle's battery and there is potential voltage drop through:

1 The vehicle's fixed wiring.
2 The relay.
3 The 12S or 13-pin cable.
4 The plug/socket interface.
5 The caravan's 12S or 13-pin cable.
6 The caravan's fixed wiring.

It means that it is a tough job to ensure 12V at the refrigerator, *but it can be done.*

WHAT CAN BE DONE?

Points 5 and 6 above are beyond the control of a towbar fitter, but the caravan maker is required to restrict the voltage drop at the connections to any fixed appliance to 0.8V and between the 12S or 13-pin plug, to the battery charger and leisure battery to 0.3V (BS EN 1648-1: 1997).

Points 3 and 4 can be significantly improved by inserting links in the caravan's 12S plug and grounding the brown wire of the 12S cable (see below). This also cures the 12S 'Pin burn-out' phenomenon.

This leaves points 1 and 2. Wiring directly to the vehicle battery with heavy duty cable (44/0.30 is the minimum recommended, but flat twin 44/0.30 or single-core 84/0.30 is better) and proper crimped connectors using ratchet type crimpers will go a long way to solving the problem. Good quality connectors and fuse holders (preferably blade type) are essential.

Voltage sensing relays (VSR) can themselves suffer nearly a 0.5V drop through the circuit board alone and the 'cycling' often witnessed, is aggravated if the 'window', i.e. the difference between the actual voltage when the relay switches in and out, is too narrow. A good VSR will have minimal drop (less than 0.2V at 20-amp load), terminal blocks large enough to handle good size cable and a broad operating window to help eliminate cycling.

You can, however, make a modification to the wiring using spare pins in order to duplicate the power and earth wiring to alleviate the voltage drop problem as well as to prevent pin burn out problems. *The modification is made to the caravan's 12S plug (and not to the socket) wiring.* As pin 5 is unused, it is possible to link pin 7 to pin 5 and (provided the brown wire is earthed in the towing vehicle) share the load between both. Additionally, as pin 2 is now unused (although still probably connected to the split charge relay) the same can be done with the feed by linking pin 6 to pin 2.

The advantages are obvious. The combination of two cores gives a greater csa than called for in the legislation and the load (feed and return) is shared by four pins instead of two. There will be less voltage drop, less resistance and less heat build up. It is a relatively simple DIY alteration and is inexpensive.

I would recommend using 28/0.30 (17.5-amp) cable for the linking wires.

When pin 5 on the 12S socket is used as an earth wire (brown) you must not connect this

with a link to pin 7 at the back of the socket and it must be wired directly to an earthing point. Earth connections must be made with a nut and bolt fastener as self-tapping screws or rivets can cause problems in service.

Although these modifications are diversions away from the standards they simply use redundant pins and make the system far more reliable and safe. These modifications came about and have been fully tested during towbar wiring courses run by the NTTA.

Info

PIN BURN-OUT

Some caravan users may find that they experience a problem with the pins and plastic moulding melting when being used. It is usually pin 6 that suffers. It can be caused by the gap in the pin's split section closing up and failing to make a good contact. This creates a point of high resistance and the pin gets hot, so hot that it will melt the plastic around the pin.

TOWING ADVICE

Many things have to be observed when towing a trailer, but it must always be driven smoothly paying full attention to your greater road presence.

7

For instance, you are driving an outfit that may be twice as long as your car and twice as heavy. This has an inevitable result on the performance and behaviour of your vehicle and it will quickly become evident that you are not able to accelerate or brake with the same results when towing. 'Allow more room' is a quote used when applied to towing, both for the width of the trailer, the length of the trailer and the distance you need for overtaking and braking. In addition you should avoid violent movements of the steering wheel or heavy braking when cornering as the response of the trailer can catch you out.

Every car has a maximum towing limit and nose weight. These should not be exceeded. If you do that you could find your insurance is nullified in the event of an accident when you make a claim. You would also be driving an overloaded vehicle and could be prosecuted under the Road Traffic Act. If you are new to towing it may be better to restrict the towing weight to the 85 per cent of the car's kerb weight level, as suggested by the caravan industry and clubs. However, this limit is a recommendation, not a law. When you are more experienced you can tow up to the limit of your car as shown in the handbook and on the VIN plate. You will need to check you have the correct driving licence category for the trailer you are about to tow. (See Chapter 2 for the regulations.)

Keep within all the rules and you will do fine: disregard them and you can be in trouble.

Choosing a towcar

If you need to change your car, as you want to tow a trailer, what should you look for? First, the car must have sufficient towing capacity – in other words its towing limit must be higher than the maximum gross weight of the trailer. The overhang should be as short as possible i.e. the distance from the centre of the rear wheel to the towball. For towing an unbraked trailer the kerb weight of the car should be at least double the maximum gross weight of the trailer. (See Chapter 2) If you are towing regularly up to the car's towing limit a turbo diesel engine would be better for its torque and fuel consumption.

Towing courses

Are you new to towing and need tuition? It can be difficult to find instruction if you want to take a B+E towing driving test as not all driving schools offer such courses. You can contact the NTTA and arrange for tuition by their provider, Towing Solutions Ltd or contact the Caravan Club or the Camping and Caravanning Club. Both clubs offer excellent training with classroom teaching followed by practical instruction in large car parks, so there are no worries about being taught on public roads. The trainers are all fully qualified driving instructors and have a simple and straightforward way of providing you with expertise. At the end of the course you will go away amazed at how

quickly you can be taught to manoeuvre a trailer or caravan. You will also take home a very practical video for additional instruction.

If you cannot get any training by a professional instructor spend some time with an experienced person and use a large industrial area out-of-hours for manoeuvring trials. If you need a B+E licence for your outfit you must display 'L' plates on the vehicle and be accompanied by a person (over 21 years of age and with two years' driving experience) who holds that category of licence. See Chapter 2 to check if you need B+E on your licence, particularly if you have a large 4x4 vehicle.

THE B+E TOWING TEST

If you passed your driving test after 1 January 1997 you will only have Category B on your licence. In order to tow outside the limits laid down for Category B licences you will have to take the B+E towing test. Those employed in the horse industry and who at some time need to drive a motorised horse box and possibly tow a trailer behind that, should consider taking a C1 driving test (a truck over 3,500kg up to 7,500kg GVW) and then a C1+E towing test. This enables you to drive a vehicle combination up to 12,000kg and you would then automatically gain B+E on your licence as well.

What is the test? For B+E you have to turn up at the test centre with a trailer having a GVW of at least 1,000kg. If your towing vehicle was first registered on or after the 1 October 2003 the following additional requirements will apply:

■ The cargo compartment of the trailer must consist of a closed box body which is at least as wide and as high as the towing vehicle; the closed box body may also be slightly less wide than the towing vehicle provided that the view to the rear is only possible by use of the external rear-view mirrors of the towing vehicle.

You will have to demonstrate, there, that you can unhitch the trailer and hitch it up again. You will be tested on reversing and braking off road at the test centre. After that you will go out on the road and drive in urban and rural areas as well as on a motorway. You will not have to demonstrate reversing during this part of the test, or emergency braking. You will have to demonstrate proficiency in driving with a longer vehicle, your placement of the vehicle on the road relative to kerbs etc. during cornering and allowing for correct vehicle spacing for braking purposes.

The EU Commission has made changes to the driving tests and candidates have to answer questions relating to vehicle safety. You will be asked questions of the 'tell me' or 'show me' type. There will be five questions in all and some examples are shown below courtesy of The Driving Standards Agency.

CAR TESTS

Candidates will be asked two questions, one 'tell me' and one 'show me'. One or both questions

answered incorrectly will result in one driving fault being recorded. Examples of safety check questions for cars:

Open the bonnet and identify (you will not have to touch any hot components just point them out)
- Where you would check the engine oil level and tell me how you would check that the engine has sufficient oil.
- Where you would check the engine coolant level and tell me how you would check that the engine has the correct level.
- Where the windscreen washer reservoir is and tell me how you would check the windscreen washer level.
- Where the brake fluid reservoir is and tell me how you would check that you have a safe level of hydraulic brake fluid.

Tell me how you would check that the:
- Brake lights are working on this car.
- Brakes are working before starting a journey.
- Tyres have sufficient tread depth and that their general condition is safe to use on the road.
- Power-assisted steering is working before starting a journey.

Show me how you would check the:
- Headlights and tail lights are working.
- Direction indicators are working.
- Horn is working (off-road only).
- Handbrake for excessive wear.

CAR + TRAILER TEST (B+E)
Drivers seeking licence entitlement for B+E should be more experienced so the assessment criteria for the category reflects this.

Candidates will be asked five questions, which will be a combination of 'show me' and 'tell me'. A driving fault will be recorded for each incorrect answer to a maximum of four.

If the candidate answers all five questions incorrectly, a serious fault will be recorded.

The following are examples of safety check questions to be used for B+E in addition to those for car tests.

'Tell me' the main safety factors involved in:
- Loading this vehicle.
- Securing a load on this vehicle.
'Show me' how you would check that:
- Your vehicle and trailer doors are secure.

UNCOUPLING AND RECOUPLING EXERCISE (B+E)
You will first have to uncouple the trailer and move your towing vehicle so that it is parked alongside it. You will then have to move the vehicle back in front of the trailer, realign it and then hitch it up. You will have to demonstrate the use of the trailer handbrake, jockey wheel and electrical connectors while doing this.

The competencies of control, accuracy and effective observation will be assessed during the exercise. A fault, which involves actual danger to the driver or another road user, will be assessed as a dangerous fault. A fault that would be potentially dangerous to the driver or another road user will be assessed as a serious fault. Faults that reflect that the driver does not have the required competencies to carry out the exercise following industry best practice and recognised procedures will be assessed as driving or serious faults, depending upon the severity of the fault.

THE MANOEUVRING TEST
The off-road part of the test begins with the examiner measuring the maximum length and width of your outfit. Traffic cones are then laid out as shown.

The distance between cones A and A1 is 1.5 times the maximum width of the outfit that you

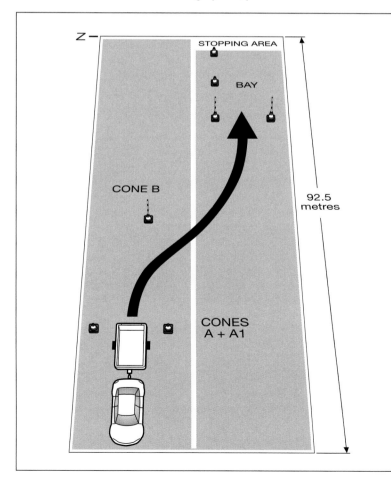

are using. The distance from cone A to cone B is twice the length of the vehicle and trailer. The distance from cone B to the end of the stopping area is three times the length of the vehicle plus trailer. The length of the 'parking bay' is at the discretion of the examiner, but will be between +1m and –2m of the length of your vehicle and trailer. There is a stopping area of 900mm at the end of the parking bay. The overall distance from start to finish is five times the length of the vehicle and trailer.

When you are successfully coupled up again, after the first part of the test, you will have to reverse the outfit from the starting point A and reverse beyond the cone at point B, keeping cone B to your right and then turn the trailer into the 'garage' space provided by the cones at point C. This must be done without hitting any of the cones. You do not have to do this in one movement. You can stop and move forward adjusting your position no more than twice. You can stop to review your position and even apply the handbrake and get out to look if necessary. Your speed should be steady, but do not go too slowly. You must end with the back of the trailer within the stopping area.

After completing these tests you will be taken out onto the road so that the examiner can see how you drive with a trailer attached. He will be looking at how you drive, allowing for the extra width and length of the outfit. If you are going to be towing a horse trailer when you have passed your test you will naturally drive the outfit with respect for the horse you are transporting and driving with gentle movements. If you drive like this in your test you will most likely fail. If, for example, you are pulling out of a minor side road onto a main carriageway you must accelerate hard to get up to the traffic speed as quickly as possible. The examiner will not want to hear that the condition of your horse is the reason for driving gently. You can adopt your driving style as appropriate after passing the test.

Hitching up

If you have a small unbraked trailer you may find it easier to take the trailer to the car as the trailer is light weight and has a relatively low nose weight. However, if the trailer is larger and you are reversing the car up to the trailer it is always easier to have someone assist you as they can indicate how close you are to the trailer, but agree on a set of hand signals first. Do not try to take a large or heavily laden trailer to the car

yourself, especially a tandem axle type as you could injure yourself as I found to my cost many years ago. Always try to hitch up on a level surface so that you do not have to operate the trailer handbrake at the same time.

Establish a pattern to work through when hitching up so that you do not drive away missing a task which could result in an accident or damage.

- First, remove the towball cover and put it in the boot. Grease the towball if needed, unless you have a friction-head stabiliser fitted, when the towball must be clean, dry, free from grease and any paint on the surface removed with emery cloth.
- If the trailer has brakes ensure that the handbrake is on. If it is on a slope it is wise to chock wheels on both sides as well.
- Release the jockey wheel clamp, lower the jockey wheel to the ground, tighten the clamp, and by turning the handle, lift up the coupling head on the trailer so that it is higher than the towball.
- If you have to move an unladen braked trailer by hand always use the jockey wheel, do not just lift the coupling up and try walking it along unless it is relatively light with a low nose weight. On tandem axle trailers you may have to use the jockey wheel to lift the front of the trailer up as high as it will go to lift the front axle off the ground to make it easier to manoeuvre by reducing tyre scrub. Always get assistance when moving large trailers.
- Position the car so that it is in line with the towball. If you have a hatchback or estate car having the rear door open may enable you to position the car more accurately. This can cause a problem on some 4x4 vehicles with side-hung rear doors, as you may not be able to shut the door without removing the jockey wheel. Lift the coupling head handle and lower the coupling head down to the towball using the jockey wheel. All modern coupling heads lock automatically to the ball. You will usually hear the click as the safety lock engages. Some couplings have a coloured button to show you that it is correctly engaged.

Safety note

Check that the head has locked onto the towball by using the jockey wheel to lift the coupling. If the back of the car starts to rise you know that it is securely connected.

- Stow the jockey wheel by first winding it up using the handle, ensuring that the fork engages in the slot in the outer tube, and then giving the handle a last extra amount of pressure to stop the wheel unwinding while you are towing. Loosen the jockey wheel clamp, lift it up fully and securely clamp it in place. For braked trailers make sure that the jockey wheel does not interfere with the brake linkage. If there is a danger that the clearance under the jockey wheel is insufficient to clear speed humps or when passing over ferry ramps you may need to remove it and store it in the car boot.
- Connect the electrical plug into the car's socket. Most commonly a seven-pin system is used known as the 12N. (See Chapter 5) The socket has a spring-assisted cover plate that is lifted to enable the connection to be made and then retains the plug in the socket. The plug can only be inserted correctly by lining up the cut-away with the lug on the socket. Leave a sufficient length of cable to enable the trailer to articulate without damaging the connection, but not too long allowing it to hit the ground. If the cable is too long you can simply twist it a few times so that it forms coils and then connect it.
- Next is a most important part of hitching up – connecting the secondary coupling. On unbraked trailers this is usually a chain but can be a loop of heavy-duty steel cable. This should be connected to an attachment point on the towbar but a loop of steel cable can only be fitted around the towball. If there is no attachment point for a chain, pass it around the towbar and secure with a 'D' shackle, or use a pigtail. (See Chapter 3.) The length of the chain needs to be sufficient to allow articulation but should not allow the coupling to hit the ground if the trailer comes off the ball.
- Braked trailers use a breakaway cable. This is a plastic-covered steel cable with a clip on the end. This should be passed around the towbar or passed through a slotted bracket and then fastened back onto itself. Do not use the clip as a direct means of attachment as it would fail before pulling the brakes on sufficiently if the trailer became detached. You can buy a 'Swedish' type clip from AL-KO Kober or BPW, which is much stronger and is of the carabiner type with interlocking teeth. This is designed to be used as the direct means of attachment. It is known as the Swedish type because that design is the one used to meet Swedish type approval regulations.

- It is not illegal to put the breakaway cable around the ball, although it is not recommended in the British Standard Code of Practice BS AU 267, particularly when used on detachable towbars. Some makes of towbar do not have any means of attaching breakaway cables other than around the towball.
- If your car has a combination type coupling, with a towing pin and a towball, do not pass the cable around the pin if the pin is part of the towball and not separate from it. If the retaining clip on that type fails, the ball, complete with pin can pull out of the coupling forging allowing the trailer to part from the car without the cable pulling the brakes on. This has resulted in fatal accidents. (See Chapter 5.)

You are now all hitched up but are you ready to go? There are still a number of things to do before moving off.

You should ensure:
- The trailer's tyre pressures are correct and the wheel bolts tightened to the required torque setting. The tyre pressures on your car may need to be increased when towing. (Check your car's handbook.)
- All the lamps work correctly.
- The nose weight is within the car manufacturer's specifications. You can purchase, quite cheaply, a nose weight gauge. This is a tubular spring balance that sits on the ground under the coupling head. The use of a piece of wood and bathroom scales works just as well. (See Loading, later in this chapter.)
- The attitude of the drawbar is correct. This is

Safety note

The drawbar should never point *up* towards the car, especially with tandem axle trailers. If it does, the rear axle could be seriously overloaded and cause bad snaking resulting in an accident. The car can be turned over and the occupants injured.

- The main cause of snaking is with large 4x4 cars when the towball is set too high for the trailer. Some have towbars where you can adjust the height of the ball to cater for this. (See Chapter 5.)

the angle of the drawbar of the trailer relative to the road surface and the car. The drawbar is the front part of the trailer, either a single tube or a vee shaped pair of side members with the coupling at the front. When the trailer is laden the drawbar should be ideally parallel with the road or facing slightly down toward the car.

■ The load is secure. Any doors or drop-down tailgate or sides are fastened and locked.

■ A numberplate is fitted to the rear of the trailer bearing the registration mark of the towing vehicle. If you need to buy one, new laws came in on 1 September 2001 where you have to show your entitlement to that registration. You will have to produce the vehicle's registration document (V5 or V5C), a photograph-type driving licence or passport, and a utility bill proving your address. If hiring a trailer make sure you have a numberplate with you or take the necessary documents with you to have a plate made by the hirer. Check that the plate you buy is the right shape for your trailer. Quite often, plates are square rather than the more common standard oblong type.

■ If any rear supports (prop stands) have been used during loading make sure that they are raised and securely clamped.

■ If any chocks have been used put them away and check the trailer's handbrake is off.

■ Sit in the driver's seat, and look in the mirrors to make sure you can see down both sides of the trailer. If you can't, you must fit mirror extensions – it's the law.

Loading a trailer

When loading a trailer it is best to do this when it is connected to the towing vehicle. If any support legs are fitted, they should be lowered to the ground and securely clamped. (See Figure 4.)

The load should be positioned equally over the axle(s) or just slightly forward in order to obtain the correct nose weight. You will have to uncouple and raise the coupling head using the jockey wheel, to check this after moving the car forward a couple of inches. The nose weight should be under the lower value of the coupling head or the towbar limit. This is the 'S' value on the towbar plate or coupling plate. If you are carrying sand or gravel, spread the load evenly over the floor – do not just pile it up at the back as the trailer might tip backwards hitting the ground with the coupling flying up towards you when unhitching. The load must be secure – it

is your legal responsibility to do this. Trailers are fitted with lashing eyes or cleats for you to tie down any loads. If your load is made up of several items put the heaviest over the axles as centrally as possible across the trailer. It is just as important to make sure that the load is not being carried to one side as it could overload the tyre(s) on that side. Keep the lightest items for putting at the front or back of the trailer.

Do you know the weight of your load? No? If you know the individual weights of each item you can simply add them together. Use your bathroom scales for smaller items if necessary. If you do not know the weights and feel you may be near the maximum limit you can tow the trailer to your nearest weighbridge and have it weighed. You will find this at your local refuse depot or at a scrap metal merchant. You must ensure you are keeping within the MGW of your trailer. The manufacturer's plate will tell you what the maximum weight is. It is very easy to keep putting items on without realising that you may be overloading your trailer and, therefore, your car. Your insurance may be declared invalid if you had an accident while towing an overloaded trailer. If you have a long item to carry you can have an overhang (See Chapter 2), but it is much better if you have a ladder rack at the front of the trailer and have the item projecting forward over the car with its other end securely located at the rear of the trailer.

You cannot use this method for tandem axle trailers however. When the trailer is loaded and coupled to the car measure the distance from the ground to a convenient point on the coupling. Then uncouple the trailer using the jockey wheel and move the car forward a few inches. Insert the nose weight gauge and then

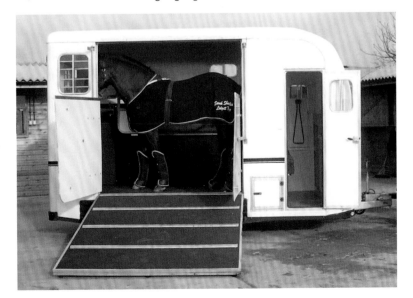

lower the drawbar using the jockey wheel until the distance from the ground is the same as it was when the trailer was coupled to the car. If you do not have a nose weight gauge you can use a set of scales and a piece of timber cut to the correct length to put the coupling at the same height from the ground. Read off the value now shown on the gauge or the scales to get the nose weight. Adjust the load if required to get within the limit. Move the car back and reconnect the trailer, not forgetting the electrical lead and secondary coupling.

Driving with a trailer

You are now all connected up and ready to go. If you are new to towing it is better to get some practice in first, at relatively low speeds using a large car park or industrial area out of hours. Note that if you hit something and cause damage to

what is private property you will be personally responsible for the damage, and will not be able to claim from your insurance company.

Reversing a trailer is usually the hardest part to learn. The bigger the trailer the easier it is, with the smallest being the most difficult. The response time for a large trailer to start to turn is relatively lengthy when compared with a small trailer – a small one seems to turn instantly. That is why you see so many people unhitch them and move them by hand. The easiest to reverse is a tandem axle trailer as tyre scrub helps in controlling the swing making it very easy to position exactly where you want it to go. A small trailer may not be visible from the driver's seat when looking through the rear window. Use the door mirrors or open the window and look out if reversing to the right. Some vehicles are fitted with a rear view camera, which can certainly help when using a small trailer.

If, for example, you want to reverse a trailer around a corner to the left you initially position the outfit in a straight line, further away from the kerb than normal as shown in Figure 1. Then, as you start to move, you turn the steering wheel to the right with your hands on the top half of the steering wheel i.e. clockwise. See Figure 2.

Then when the trailer has turned sufficiently to the left you begin to turn the steering wheel the opposite way i.e. to the left, anticlockwise, to allow the car to follow the trailer. See Figure 3.

(If you delay this action you can cause the outfit to jack-knife and may damage the bodywork of the car as it can collide with the trailer.) You now straighten up with the steering wheel until the outfit is now in a straight line around the corner, as in Figure 4. Practice makes perfect.

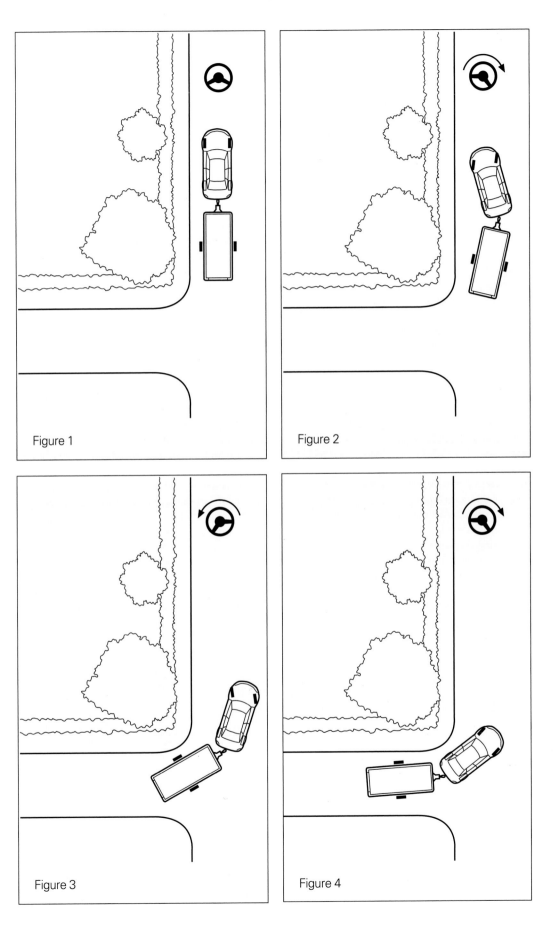

Figure 1

Figure 2

Figure 3

Figure 4

Have a look at the NTTA website www.ntta.co.uk for a moving diagram of the reversing process.

Driving in a forward direction is much easier. Simply drive a little further away from the edge of the road if your trailer is wider than your car and allow more space between you and the car in front of you for a greater braking distance. This is especially so for unbraked trailers as your brakes may have to cope with a 50 per cent heavier weight. Be more gentle with your actions on the controls, avoiding any sudden applications of the brakes when turning a corner.

When turning to the left make sure that when you enter the turn you do so a little later than normal so the front of the car is further away from the kerb, as the trailer wheels do not follow in the exact path of the car's wheels – they 'cut' the corner.

Take particular care when turning right across the path of oncoming traffic, as they may not see you have a trailer attached to the rear of your vehicle.

Safety note

When turning right from a side road on to a dual carriageway road remember that your outfit is much longer and you do not want to stop in the centre of the carriageway with your trailer sticking out into the overtaking lane of the road you are crossing. Lives have been lost through this action.

Should you ever be towing at the limit of your car, its performance will be reduced and you may find you are collecting a queue of cars behind you. If you see that this is happening pull into the first lay-by you come to and let the traffic past. It will not delay you more than a couple of minutes and exhibits a courteous manner to other road users. Failure to do this could involve you in an accident if an impatient driver attempts to overtake where they shouldn't.

Try to read the road ahead with a towing frame of mind and when you approach a hill, change down a gear a little earlier than normal to keep your speed up. Take great care when going down a hill. This is the situation where most towing accidents occur. In this instance you have the trailer pushing the back of the car.

You should reduce speed when going down hills, selecting a lower gear if necessary, taking note of any cross winds, particularly on motorways. If you see a fluorescent pink windsock, take care. It is there to indicate the strength of any crosswind.

Keep an eye out for lorries that pull out to overtake you. The front of the lorry will cause a bow wave of air that will push the back of your trailer to the nearside and when the back of the lorry passes you the vortex causes the trailer to be pulled the opposite way. This can cause a snake to occur with larger box van trailers and caravans more susceptible to this than normal, general-purpose trailers.

Towing with different types of trailer

Some trailers have special requirements that differ from a normal trailer and have their own towing needs to be considered.

Livestock and horse trailers demand a driving style that takes into account that your load is alive. You would not want to arrive at a point-to-point with a horse suffering from travel sickness. Take it steady when accelerating or braking and try to be smooth in your driving style. Horses are surprisingly heavy with a high centre of gravity and can move around a little, so do not rush around corners. Remember that when you stop for refreshment on a journey your animals will also need some too, and there are laws relating to the carriage of livestock (regarding space and refreshment), relevant to journey times.

Boat trailers also suffer from high centre of

gravity when laden and a sailing yacht with a fixed keel will have the hull of the boat way up in the air. This has to be taken into account in your driving style. Side winds can affect handling considerably and take particular care on roads in exposed areas.

If the trailer was not built especially for the boat it may have axles that can be moved along the frame. Adjust the axle positions to get the correct nose weight. Powerboats often have outboard motors on the stern. This is a lot of weight in the most inappropriate place. If a snake starts in this situation the 'pendulum effect' can take over with alarming consequences. The axles will need to be moved further back in order to compensate for the weight of the motor.

Safety note

When launching a boat from a trailer, do not reverse into the water immediately on arrival. The trailer hubs will be hot and if you put them into cold water a vacuum will be formed in the hub and bearings causing water to be sucked in past the oil seals. This can cause serious damage to the bearing surfaces and can be very costly to put right. It can cause a hub to seize up while towing, with dangerous results. Some axles are made with pressurised hubs to prevent this happening.

Snaking

Snaking is the most frightening situation that you can get into when towing. This is when the trailer or caravan starts to move from side to side with excessive movements. It is quite normal to experience a small side-to-side movement when other vehicles overtake you but these will settle down almost immediately. If a bad snake occurs the side-to-side motion can become very violent, with large degrees of movement and can result in the trailer jack-knifing and even overturning. The design of some couplings restrict the rotary movement of the coupling head on the ball to 25° either side of vertical, so if the trailer overturns it can take the car with it and result in serious injury to the occupants. Other designs allow the coupling head to rotate through 360° so the worst that can happen is for the trailer to lift the back of the car off the ground, and should not result in serious injury to the occupants.

Many things can cause snaking:
- Being overtaken by heavy lorries.
- A badly loaded trailer with incorrect nose weight, or more weight on one side than the other.
- Incorrect tyre pressures.
- Drawbar pointing up towards the towcar.
- Driving too fast downhill with crosswinds.

If a snake occurs, do not try braking hard to correct it. Just take your foot off the accelerator and position it on the brake pedal, without applying any pressure and, holding the steering wheel reasonably firmly, steer it in a straight line allowing the outfit to gently slow down. Most trailers will become stable again quite quickly. Do not try to steer your way out of a snake. You will never time your steering wheel movements correctly and will only make things worse. Also, do not attempt to accelerate out of a snake. Your car's power-to-weight ratio will never be big enough to let you do that. Should you experience snaking often, do not think that fitting a stabiliser will cure the problem. Examine the trailer and its load, the tyre pressures, the nose weight and the drawbar angle. A stabiliser will not cure a badly set up trailer. It will only help a well set up trailer to overcome the bow wave

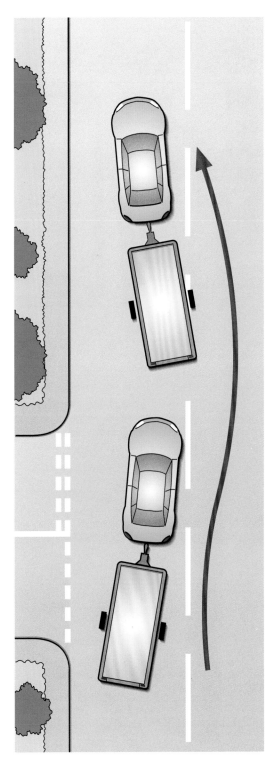

problems, crosswind situations and instability caused by bad road surfaces such as the grooves worn into the road surface by large lorries on the inside lane of many motorways. (See Chapter 5, for stabilisers.)

In general terms, if you drive smoothly within the limits of your car the safer will be your journey.

MAINTAINING AND SERVICING YOUR TRAILER

Trailers can be the most abused vehicles on the road. In general they are left standing around for weeks at a time then simply hitched up and used without any thought of maintenance whatsoever.

8

As you cannot drive a trailer you do not know immediately of any faults as you do when driving a car. This is why a trailer should be serviced annually as well as the subject of routine checks and simple maintenance tasks during the year. Look after your trailer and it will save you a lot of money in replacing parts; regular maintenance will mean trouble-free towing enabling you to complete journeys safely. If you do not feel confident to carry out maintenance on braked trailers, not forgetting that automatic reversing brakes are unique and require careful adjustment, then book your trailer in to your local trailer centre for this work to be done by a professional.

Unbraked trailers

On those trailers not fitted with brakes the number of items requiring servicing is reduced considerably.

Starting at the front the coupling head requires checking for wear, cleaning and lubricating.

First, clean out the old grease using a solvent such as white spirit and then after letting it dry, apply fresh general-purpose extreme pressure (EP) grease to *DIN Standard 51825*. The head must be greased to prevent wear either in the head or on the towball. Some heads have 'wear' indicators, usually markings on the sides of the head or on a Bradley coupling by the slot in the release catch, as seen below.

If the position of the handle shows that it is on or near the maximum wear level you can insert a new 50mm ball and see what effect this has on the wear indicator level. If the wear indicator moves back to the correct level then your towball is worn. If the level reads the same as before then your coupling head is worn. Change whatever components are worn to prevent the trailer coming off the towball while towing. Ensure that the coupling mounting bolts are tight.

Check that the secondary coupling safety chain (or heavy-duty steel cable loop) is in good condition and its retaining bolt is secure.

The hubs will be either of the no-maintenance self-sealed type or will have grease nipples allowing lubrication. On the latter type pump in high-melting point (HMP) grease every 3,000miles or six months, whichever is the sooner.

The spaces above and below the handle show the amount of wear.

Check all bolts for tightness and tighten where required. If you need access to the underside most small, unbraked trailers can be stood on end making it easy to reach the nuts and bolts.

While you have the trailer in this position check the wiring for any damage; if it has become unclipped refasten as required. If the trailer is of the tipping type make sure that the release knob is fully screwed down.

One item that does get damaged easily is the seven-pin electrical plug. If your trailer has a fitting to hold the plug when the trailer is not being towed please get into the habit of using it as it is very easy to damage the commonly found plastic-type plugs if left dangling. Check the plug for damage and occasionally remove the side screws allowing access to the wiring connections and tighten all seven wiring screws ensuring good contacts are made.

Braked trailers

COUPLING HEAD

The coupling head is serviced as for the unbraked trailer above. The difference now is that the coupling is bolted to the drawshaft of an overrun device. It is quite common for the overrun device to be described as 'the coupling or hitch'. If the coupling head is bolted onto the drawshaft check the fixing bolts for tightness. You may find that the coupling is fastened on with 'keepit & cappit' fasteners where no bolt head or nuts are showing. This is an anti-theft fastener and is covered in Chapter 9.

If you need to change the head it is *not* simply removed by undoing the two bolts as one end of the damper may be held by one of these bolts and the damper could very rapidly extend fully. (Note that on some couplings a pin holds the damper between the two retaining bolts.) To remove the retaining bolt holding the damper you take off the nut and then gently tap out the bolt using a round pin, of the same diameter as the bolt. It should also be long enough to retain the damper but not long enough to prevent removal of the coupling

head. This pin will stay within the drawshaft retaining the damper when the head is removed. When refitting a new head simply tap the retaining bolt through the head and shaft thus knocking out this retaining pin. Fit new self-locking nuts; *never reuse the old nuts, as these are safety critical items.* Torque the nuts up to 100Nm for M12 or 125Nm for M14 bolts. If you do fit new bolts they should be to 10.9 grade and these numbers will be stamped on the head of the bolts.

OVERRUN DEVICE

The overrun device is fitted with a damper to control the rate of application of the brakes. They used to be filled only with hydraulic fluid but most are now gas or oil-filled. They can be tested, after applying the handbrake fully, by pushing the head in to see how much resistance they show to the force you are transmitting. If the damper shows resistance over the length of travel and then, when released, slowly extends back to its fully out position then the damper is working correctly. If it goes in easily when you push and it does not return or returns very rapidly, then it is faulty and needs to be replaced.

With heavy trailers it can be difficult to push the drawshaft in due to the necessary high internal pressure of the damper. In this case use a lashing strap made into a loop and put this around the coupling head and the rear of the overrun device's body as seen below.

With this in place, use the ratchet handle to pull the coupling head into the overrun device until no further movement takes place. Then

release the ratchet handle and the damper should slowly push the head back until the drawshaft is fully extended.

A rubber boot protects the drawshaft and it must be kept located on the head and the body of the overrun device. Replace the boot if it is split following the instructions for the damper replacement up to the point where you are able to remove the coupling head. The drawshaft should be checked for any damage before fitting a new boot. Secure the boot with new cable pull-ties.

To change the damper follow the instructions below but please take care when handling dampers and disposing of them. ***Warning:*** *The damper is pre-loaded and compressed in order for the coupling to operate correctly, so do not stand immediately in front of or to the rear of the damper in case it fails during the removal or fitting.*

REMOVAL OF A DAMPER

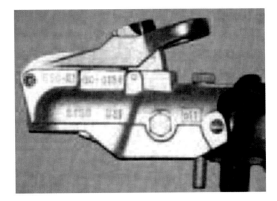

- Pull back the rubber boot from the coupling head, cutting the nylon cable pull-tie if fitted, to expose the securing bolts.
- Undo the self-locking nut from the rear bolt and then remove the bolt. Force may be needed to free the bolt if it is the front mounting bolt for the damper and the damper is still preloaded.
- When this bolt is removed the damper will move forward to rest against the front bolt unless it is of the type with a separate retaining pin.
- If it has the separate retaining pin remove the front coupling bolt enabling you to remove the coupling head. Replace both coupling bolts through the drawshaft and finger-tighten the nuts. Knock out the retaining pin and then remove the rear bolt. This will now allow the damper to move forward and rest against the front bolt as in step 3.
- From underneath you must now drill a 3mm

diameter hole into the damper body tube to a depth of 8mm to allow the gas to escape.

Warning: *You must observe normal safety precautions when using power tools, especially if out of doors, and wear safety glasses. Do not lie immediately underneath the bolt hole when drilling as gas will escape when the drill enters the damper body.*

The gas pressure should now have been released so the front bolt can now be removed. If there is difficulty in removing this bolt there may still be some gas pressure in the damper. You should repeat step 5 and drill a further hole in the damper body.

Remove the rear damper mounting and then remove the nut and spring washer from the end of the damper rod.

The de-pressurised damper can now be removed by sliding it forwards through the drawshaft.

It is advisable to drain the remaining oil from the old damper before disposing of it. To drain the oil drill a 3mm diameter hole in the damper body 60mm from the damper rod end. Dispose of the oil in the appropriate waste tank at your nearest waste disposal centre.

REPLACING A DAMPER

Slide in the new damper and re-fit the head ensuring the rear bolt goes through the front damper eye or the separate retaining pin locates and secures the damper.

Fit the rear damper mounting bracket to the damper rod.

The damper now has to be compressed to align the mounting bracket with its two mounting holes. **Warning:** *Proceed with extreme caution.*

Compress the damper using a suitable lever until the two holes in the mounting bracket line up with the holes in the rear of the main casting

and drop in the retaining bolts. Fit the nuts and torque up to the settings shown above in the coupling head section.

Jockey wheel and propstands

There are two types of jockey wheel: the lighter weights ones have a plain tube and the heavier types a ribbed tube.

The lighter ones are usually fitted through a mounting hole in the main overrun body casting and the heavier type are fitted to the side of the drawbar with a clamp. Both types have a pad

fitted between the clamp handle and the tube. Do not use a jockey wheel without this clamp, as the surface of the tube will be damaged.

You will find that some have two small slots in the base of the outer tube for the wheel fork to sit in when fully wound up to prevent the wheel from coming down while travelling. Check to ensure that these slots are not damaged. The other way of preventing the jockey wheel from working loose is to have an 'R' clip or spring loaded pin at the top of the tube locking the handle to the tube. Make sure that the clip is fitted and secure on its chain or the pin is properly located.

There are two types of clamp used: one-piece and two-piece. The two pieces should be adjusted so that there is a gap between both parts on the fixed side with all movement taken up by the handle side.

The jockey wheel should be fully unwound and the screw thread lubricated with oil, such as 3-In-One. Lubricate the wheel spindle at the same time. This should be done a couple of times a year.

Rear propstands come in two designs either a plain tube or one with a screw adjustable foot.

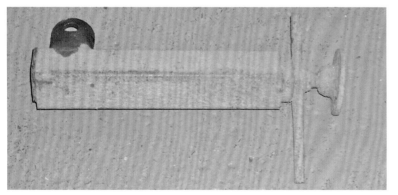

These can seize-up if not regularly screwed out and lubricated.

The one shown had to be heated up with an oxygen/acetylene torch, given copious applications of penetrating oil and considerable muscle power to free it off before it was fit for service.

Breakaway cable

The breakaway cable needs to be checked to see it is in good condition without any signs of fraying or damage to the plastic covering. See that the flat spring blade in the clip is not permanently deformed leaving a gap for it to

come off while travelling. The spring strip should be in contact with the underside of the hook. Make sure that the cable is fitted through a guide underneath the coupling or it cannot do its job properly if the trailer becomes detached.

You can replace the breakaway cable with the Swedish type from AL-KO Kober which has a swivelling section with teeth that engage in the main hook part of the clip, replacing the flat spring strip, in the manner of climber's carabiner clips. The pivot point of this type of clip will need to be lubricated twice a year.

The brakes

The main area of work on trailers is related to the braking system. The brakes will need regular checking but it is very difficult to give a service interval for maintaining trailer brakes. However, they should be done at least once a year. To know if they do need adjustment you can push in the coupling head/drawshaft and see how far it moves into the overrun device. Modern overrun devices have around 90–100mm of movement. If the shaft moves more than 45mm then the brakes should be adjusted. Another indication of the brakes' condition can be given by the use of the handbrake lever. First, make sure that the brake shoes are not in the reversing position by first reversing the trailer and then pulling the car forward about 600mm (2ft) so that the coupling shaft is fully extended. Now pull the handbrake on and see if the trailer can be moved in both a forwards and reverse direction. If it moves in either direction the system needs adjusting. Now you need to see if the handbrake holds the trailer when the lever is applied with the brake shoes in the automatic reversing position. Apply the handbrake and see if the trailer can be moved rearwards. Note that when trying the reverse direction the trailer may roll back a little way due to the automatic reversing system operating. It should then be held by the handbrake as extra force will be applied by the energy stored in the spring box fitted in the brake linkage. This causes the handbrake lever to rise more to the vertical. If it does the automatic reversing system is working correctly as the spring energy has overcome the extra movement needed to ensure the brake shoes are in full contact with the drum. The trailer should now be unable to move any further backwards or forwards. If there is still wheel movement then the brake system requires adjusting to take up any free play in the linkage. Follow the adjustment procedure shown later in this chapter.

All brake manufacturers have automatic reversing brake systems, which are very similar in principle. Knott and AL-KO make the most commonly found brakes. Details of how to strip and rebuild Knott brakes are shown later in this chapter and where other makes have variations these will be indicated accordingly.

REPLACING BRAKE SHOES

It is advisable to remove the hubcap first, as shown, to see what type of bearings are fitted. If they are taper roller bearings with the hub held in place with a castellated nut

Castellated nut and split pin on taper roller bearing hub.

and split pin then you can carry on as instructed below.

If it is a plain hub nut then the replacement nut has to be tightened to 350Nm/260lb ft (AL-KO 290Nm/215lb ft) which is a very high torque that requires a torque wrench of a size not usually owned by a DIY person. Make sure that you can borrow or hire one before proceeding.

The trailer must be jacked up but before lifting the trailer, loosen the wheel nuts/bolts *but do not remove them.* Support the axle on axle stands; *do not rely on jacks alone. If the jack is on tarmac you should use a support plate,* either steel or of strong plywood, under the jack when raising the trailer. Similar plates must be used under the axle stands in order to spread the load and prevent them sinking into the tarmac. If you can only work on one side at a time you must chock the wheels still on the ground as well as the jockey wheel to stop the trailer from rolling. The handbrake lever should be in the fully off position and if it is of the over-centre or gas strut-assisted type it must be locked in the off position. Knott supply a handbrake locking bolt for this with a red finish as shown here.

If you do not have the bolt then the handbrake lever can be tied down with strong rope. The reason for this is that when you are adjusting the front part of the linkage you may inadvertently cause the handbrake lever to operate and it can come up quickly and hit you in the face causing injury.

After lifting the trailer and having supported it safely.

Remove the wheels. Place them under the trailer for extra security while working on the brakes.

Remove the hubcap using the tip of a screwdriver as shown here.

Remove the axle nut. If it is a castellated nut remove the split pin first.

Remove the drum. You may need the use of a hub puller, taking care not to displace the roller bearings, as they do tend to fall out. Placing a cloth under the hub will prevent dirt getting into the bearings if you do drop them.

Check the condition of the braking surface of the drum. This is the area that the brake shoes contact when in use. If it is badly scored replace the drum.

Undo the locknut on the brake rod that runs along the centre of the trailer and then slacken off its adjacent nut. This will allow you to pull the brake cable outer casing away from the backplate allowing the half shell to be removed.

Slacken off the brake adjuster bolt on the backplate until free. (Note that some brakes are adjusted by a ratchet or starwheel accessed through a hole in the backplate or through the front face of the drum.)

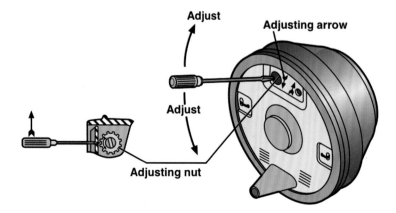

Adjust

Adjusting arrow

Adjust

Adjusting nut

Detach the brake cable from the expander mechanism.

Check the position of the shoes and springs on the backplate to ensure that you replace them in the same position. See below for a view of the nearside assembly, the offside being a mirror image of this. Note that the upper shoe with a plain web is the leading shoe. A web is the backbone of the brake shoe at right angles to the friction material's backing plate. The lower, trailing, shoe with the two-piece web is known as the sliding shoe. It is recommended that you take a photograph of the original assembly so that you can use it to refer to when reassembling the brakes. (Digital photography is ideal for this sort of job.)

Carefully, using a suitable lever if necessary, lift the sliding shoe away from the expander and then remove the expander from the backplate.

Remove the central retaining spring from the leading shoe taking care to retain the spring as well as the pin at the rear of the backplate.

Lift off the whole brake shoe assembly from the backplate, taking care not to lose the two adjuster wedges fitted into the brake adjuster situated at the end of the brake shoes opposite the expander.

2 Locate the shoes on to the backplate and position the adjuster block ensuring that the adjuster wedges are in place.

3 Refit the retaining spring on the leading shoe.

The sliding shoe can now be removed from its carrier by releasing the two springs.

Check all components to be reused and replace any that are damaged. Clean the expander mechanism and all other parts with a brush or cloth, *but do not lubricate them. Brakes create heat and any grease applied can melt and get onto the friction material seriously reducing braking performance.*

REFITTING SHOES AND ADJUSTING THE BRAKES

1 Refit the springs to the new shoes. The sliding shoe is clearly marked showing the direction of the drum rotation enabling you to fit it the correct way round.

Tip

Note: You must change brake shoes in axle sets. *Never* change brake shoes on one side only.

4 Position the expander on the leading shoe.

5 With care, using an appropriate lever on the sliding shoe, position the expander between the shoes.

6 The expander is now ready to receive the brake cable.

7 The brake cable can now be fitted and the half shell put in place securing it by sliding the outer cable collar over its end. If the cable shows signs of wear, stiffness, damage or fraying it should be replaced with a new one.

8 The drum can now be refitted.

9 If it is of the plain axle nut design refit the washer and tighten the nut to the trailer maker's designated torque and then, using a punch, hammer the collar into one of the axle grooves to lock the nut.

You may, with this make of axle, use the nut for a second time punching in the collar opposite the first position. If both grooves have previously been used you must use a new nut. **Note:** If it is an AL-KO axle you can only use a nut once! A new one must always be used. Due to the high torque settings of axle nuts I would always recommend that you use a new one every time a hub is removed. Then fit the hubcap. **Note:** On hubs with sealed bearings do not put any grease in the cap.

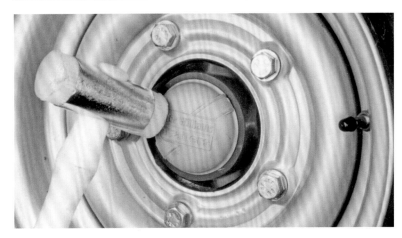

10 If it has a taper roller bearing then make sure that it has an adequate amount of HMP grease in the rollers and tighten to 70Nm while slowly turning the drum. Then slacken off the nut and whilst holding the drum steady tighten the nut using only your fingers. Then back off the nut until the split pin hole in the axle lines up with the first castellation slot you come to and insert a new split pin and fold it over the end of the axle to secure the nut as shown earlier, 'Replacing brake shoes'. With taper roller bearings you can put grease in the hubcap.

11 Repeat for all the other brakes.

12 Check the wheels for any damage to the rims.

13 Check the tyres for any damage, cuts or cracking of the sidewalls and in the bottom of the tread grooves. Check the age of the tyre from the date code on the sidewalls. If over five years old and there are signs of cracking in the tread grooves replace the tyre even if there appears to be plenty of tread depth left remaining.

Tyre damaged due to running flat

14 Re-fit all the wheels.

15 Adjust the brakes as shown below.

ADJUSTING THE BRAKES

If you are following on from replacing the brake shoes then the trailer will already be raised and safely supported. If not, the trailer needs to be raised following the instructions given at the beginning of the 'Replacing the brake shoes' section earlier.

The braking system must always be adjusted starting at the brakes and working forward. *Never try adjusting the brakes from the handbrake end. You may cause the handbrake to come on while towing, with the possibility of very expensive damage as a result.* With tandem axle trailers start with the rear axle brakes first.

Ensure that the overrun device's drawshaft is fully extended. If it isn't, check that the damper is working correctly. See above section on couplings and overrun devices.

Make sure that the handbrake lever is in the fully 'off' position and locked down using the locking bolt or is securely tied down. (If you have a trailer with the older style B&B Sigma coupling the extra stored energy is provided by large springs inside the brake drum so the handbrake linkage is not affected.)

Turn the wheel in a forward rotary direction only. *You must never rotate the wheel in the reverse direction whilst adjusting the brakes.* Turn the brake adjuster bolt in a clockwise direction until resistance is felt when the brake shoes contact the drum. Slowly turn the adjuster bolt anticlockwise until the wheel begins to rotate freely again. If your brake has a starwheel or ratchet adjuster move it a click at a time until the resistance is felt and then back off until the wheel moves freely.

Repeat for the other brakes.

Adjusting the brakes will have altered the setting on the brake rod and compensator. Turn the brake rod nut until it just meets the compensator crossbar, as seen in the illustration in step 7. in the section on replacing brake shoes. ***Warning:*** *Do not overtighten this nut or you will cause brake drag, resulting in overheating of the hubs.* Then lock this nut in place with the adjacent locknut.

Remove the handbrake locking bolt and operate the handbrake several times to ensure that all the brake shoes are centred in the drums and the compensators are seated. Check the travel of the brake cables at the compensator. This should be 2–5mm. If not, readjust the brakes accordingly.

With the handbrake engaged turn each wheel in the reverse direction. They should rotate a little, as the reverse mechanism is

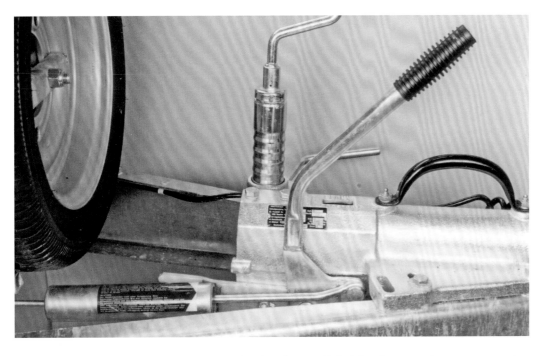

actuated, and then lock. As you turn each wheel there will be a small upward movement of the handbrake lever as the energy stored by the spring in the spring box, the red cylinder, (situated just behind the handbrake) adds the extra pull needed to take account of the brake shoe movement.

Each wheel should lock but if one does not then there is too much slack in the system. The adjustment of that brake should be redone.

Have a look at the compensator to see if the crossbar is at right angles to the brake rod. If not it can be corrected by adjusting the appropriate brake cable(s). This is often required if a replacement cable has been fitted. To ensure equal braking forces the compensator crossbar must be at right angles to the brake rod.

The brake rod, if unsupported, can move up and down while the trailer is in motion and this movement can cause the brakes to be applied intermittently so check that the brake rod supports are doing their job. Supports can be simply metal brackets with a clearance hole for the rod to pass through or flexible straps. On tandem axles the brake rod should be extended so that it is supported in a clearance hole in the brake cable bracket on the front axle.

Now apply the handbrake and lower the trailer back on to the ground.

Check the tightness of the wheel bolts/nuts.

ROAD TESTING AND BEDDING IN NEW BRAKE SHOES

You can now take the trailer out for a road test and try the brakes. *Always take care that there is no vehicle following you when you are testing the brakes.* It is advisable to take someone with you to observe the behaviour of the trailer when you apply the brakes.

Ideally, drive on a level road at 20–25mph and apply the brakes gradually to make a smooth stop. How did the trailer behave when braking? If it stepped out of line due to one side braking harder than the other the brake adjustment must be checked. Look particularly at the setting of the compensator crossbar. Adjust until you achieve smooth straight line braking. If you have to readjust the brakes after testing them allow time for the drums to cool down before doing so, *as they will be hot.*

Then drive again at the higher speed of 35–40mph and apply the brakes firmly, without locking up the wheels, to see if the trailer still pulls up in a straight line. If satisfactory, go out again and drive at 50–55mph, obviously on a road that permits that speed, to ensure that the brakes still pull the trailer up smoothly in a straight line.

The important thing during these tests is for a gradual build up of the braking forces, avoiding very gentle braking or sudden high-pressure braking. Gentle braking can glaze the linings resulting in a loss of brake power. Current laws now require all brake linings to be made of asbestos-free materials. This makes them more prone to sticking to the drums if the trailer is parked, with the handbrake on, for long periods. You should always try to leave a trailer parked without the brakes on and with the wheels chocked to prevent movement. You should also

ensure that if you have reversed a trailer into its parking position that you pull forward slightly after reversing to allow the brake shoes to be in their normal 'forward' position.

If you find that the shoes have stuck to the drums then you should slacken off the brakes by turning the adjuster bolt anticlockwise about half a turn. Then, using a soft faced (rubber, leather or wooden) mallet, as shown being used to refit the hub cap on page 119, tap the bottom of the brake backplate. If this action does not release the brakes then jack up the trailer, supporting it securely, and remove the wheels. Tap the brake drums with the mallet and this should release the shoes. Refit the wheels and adjust the brakes before using the trailer. Lower the trailer back down and torque up the wheel bolts.

It will take at least 500 miles of driving on normal roads (not motorways, as there is normally very little braking while travelling on them) to fully bed-in new linings.

If a trailer has been left standing for a long period make sure that no parts of the braking system have seized before using it. Grease all moving parts in the system with EP grease.

Electrical

- Inspect the seven-pin plug for damage and replace if necessary.
- Check that the electrical cable has not been dragging on the road while towing and has worn through the outer cover. Replace if it has.
- Check the operation of the lights and condition of the lenses. If any fail to work check the condition of the bulb and if that is OK then check the condition of the contacts in the bulb holder. These are prone to corrosion and should be cleaned and protected with a smear of Vaseline.
- Check that the front, side and rear reflectors are still fitted and have not fallen off. Replace any missing ones.

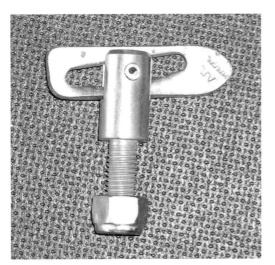

Bodywork and fittings

- Check all nuts and bolts for tightness. If there is a drop-down tailgate check the retaining catches (droplocks) for wear. If there is no gap showing in the slot when the tailgate is fastened the droplock is worn and could vibrate into the release position while travelling. Replace if they are found to be in this condition.
- If there is glass-reinforced plastic bodywork check for cracks or crazing in the surface, especially in the corners. You will often find cracking where a roller shutter door is fitted. Repair any defects found. For crazing repairs you must sand back the top surface and apply a new gel coat.
- Check the condition of the floor, especially on horse trailers. These floors are subjected to urine and can deteriorate to the point where a horse can fall through when the trailer is being towed, with terrible injuries to the animal. Try pushing the blade of a screwdriver into the floor in random places both from the top and bottom. If any soft areas are found take the trailer to the nearest dealer and have it examined properly to see if a replacement floor is required. Replacing a horse trailer floor is a job is best left to experts, especially as there has been a change from timber laminates to metal floors over the past few years and most horse trailer makers have made replacement conversion kits.
- Occasionally, a spring can break on a horse trailer's rear ramp. Do not use it in this condition; ramps are heavy and can cause injury because one spring will not support the weight. Replace the spring before using again.

Wheels and tyres

- Check the condition of the tyres as described in steps 12 and 13 of the 'Replacing brake shoes' section. Wear strong leather gloves whilst checking the sidewalls in case any strands of steel wire from the reinforcing plies are protruding from the tyre.
- Check the pressures and adjust as necessary. The pressure setting is moulded into the sidewall of the tyre. Some tyres have an allowance for 10% extra loading for speeds not exceeding 60mph and require a higher pressure. Consult your trailer maker for the required tyre pressures.
- Check the wheels for damage both sides. They can be damaged through kerbing i.e. clipping the wheel against a kerb by not allowing enough distance for the trailer's 'cut in' when cornering.
- If you are leaving the trailer parked for some time it should be jacked up with the wheels off the ground.
- Cover the wheels with a light-proof bag, while the trailer is left unused for long periods – a black plastic sack is ideal. This prevents the tyre's sidewall from being damaged by ultra violet rays from the sun.
- Do not forget the spare, which is commonly left exposed at all times to the sun. It may be years before being used, as punctures are not very common these days. It should always be covered as it can be damaged enough to fail when used as a replacement.

SECURITY PRODUCTS FOR YOUR TRAILER

No matter how much you value your trailer there is always someone who values it more, but is not prepared to pay you for it.

Trailer theft is very common and you need to take precautions to hold on to yours. These can be in the form of physical barriers, electronic methods and simply the way you use it.

All security systems cost money and you have to take into account the value of the trailer and the consequences of its loss, when deciding how much to spend and what forms of security are appropriate. Your insurance provider will also tell you what their minimum security requirements are: usually a hitchlock and a wheel clamp.

Physical security

The most common products are hitchlocks. Some makes of trailer coupling have a lock built into the head and this can be used when parked, or while towing the trailer.

Unfortunately, thieves can drill out these locks so many trailer owners also fit a hitchlock which covers the entire coupling head as well as the head's retaining bolts. If the head is held on by bolts, thieves can simply remove the head by unbolting it and substituting it with one that they have brought with them.

Some trailer makers use pins and hardened caps, called 'Keepit and Capit' instead of retaining bolts, which have to be drilled out to remove them. This task takes a thief much longer and it can make a lot of noise which might attract people's attention.

The really 'professional' thieves can overcome this form of security by having a 'drop box' mounted on the back of their vehicle

and they simply lift the front of the trailer and drop it into this box, lash it down and drive away. It is necessary, therefore, to prevent a trailer from being movable. The first way is to fit a wheel clamp and these devices come in many forms. The really heavy-duty ones are designed to fit around the tyre and cover all the wheel bolts so that the wheel, complete with clamp, cannot be removed.

The other design is a 'U'-shaped fabrication that goes around the tyre and fits onto a modified wheel stud and is retained in that position by a built-in lock. An example of this design is the SAS Supaclamp Gold.

When choosing a wheel clamp check its weight as some are very heavy and may prove particularly cumbersome to fit. There are also big differences in the quality of wheel clamps and there are test standards for these products, which are described later in this chapter.

Another way to prevent a trailer from being moved by an unauthorised person is to use a ground anchor. These take the form of a steel fixture set into a concrete base and a have heavy-duty chain which is then used to fasten the trailer to the anchor.

Obviously, the strength of the system depends on the quality of the anchor and the amount of concrete around it; the bigger the 'lump' of concrete the better. If you already have a concrete drive or base the anchor can take the form of a pin which is chemically glued

into a predrilled hole in the concrete. The strength of this installation can be quite incredible and it can be very difficult, if not impossible, to remove a fixture from the ground, but an anchor is only as good as the chain and its padlock.

The chain should be made from hardened steel and its links have a minimum diameter of 13mm, preferably 16mm, although it will then be quite heavy to handle. The chain has to be passed around the chassis members and secured with the highest quality of padlock that you can afford. If you have the anchor situated underneath the trailer it is especially difficult for a thief to work there with an angle grinder or hydraulic cutters. With the anchor in this position it can also be awkward to fit the chain, but it is worth the discomfort for the security and peace of mind which it provides.

Another strategy is to put a barrier of steel posts around a trailer's parking place using a locking post at the front to allow access. This post can have a 50mm towball fixed to the top to which the trailer can be secured.

Yet another form of physical security is named the 'Supermule'. This is a swing down arm that digs itself into the ground if a trailer is moved.

Alarms and tracking systems

Alarm systems are available for trailers fitted with bodywork incorporating doors, e.g. horse or box van trailers. These operate by setting off a very loud alarm when a door is opened. They also incorporate a tilt sensor that sets off the alarm when the front of the trailer is lifted to couple it up to the towing vehicle. These can be effective if the trailer is situated close to your house, but as with any audible alarms, is dependent on someone taking action upon hearing it. Moreover, 98 per cent of all alarms activated are false, so do not rely too heavily on this form of security – simply use one as an extra form of protection to frighten away a thief. Also, do not rely on the Police responding to this type of alarm as they have many priorities that will come before yours. Most alarms are powered by a battery and since its life is limited it must be checked at regular intervals and replaced when necessary. One neat system is the SPA (solar-powered alarm) from DES Locksmiths which solves the problem of battery life. Some types can also have a GSM (global system for mobile communications) 'pay-as-you-go subscriber identity module (SIM) card' fitted so that you can be called on your telephone informing you that an attempt is being made to steal your trailer.

In addition, there are tracking systems which can be incorporated into an alarm system or used covertly. Since they need battery power they can be used on exhibition or hospitality trailers that will usually have a leisure battery on board. A 'proactive' tracking system is an onboard global positioning system (GPS) which sets up a 'geofence' (a five-metre circle) around the trailer. If your trailer moves outside that circle the tracker activates itself and sends you or a tracking company details that it is moving, together with information about its exact location. The position can be shown on your own home computer or you can have the tracking provider do this for you. The better tracker providers notify the Police or use a recovery company. (The Police may not be able to respond as fast as you would like.)

A tracking company should have agreements with Police forces but not all have these in place, so find out if the ones you are looking at have arrangements or not. Phantom Ltd, for example, has both proactive and target tracking systems and an arrangement with the Police. It uses 24 GPS satellites to obtain a very accurate location of your trailer and this, along with your Police crime number is used to engage the services of the local Constabulary. The Police do not need any onboard equipment in their cars so can use the nearest Officers to go to the location. This system is Thatcham 'Q' listed and has a Sold Secure Gold (see later section on product quality) with Control Centre rating. Details can be found on www.phantom.uk.net. Tracking systems usually have an initial cost followed up with annual subscriptions. Obviously, your trailer would have to be quite valuable before it merits having such a system installed.

SPA solar-powered alarm system.

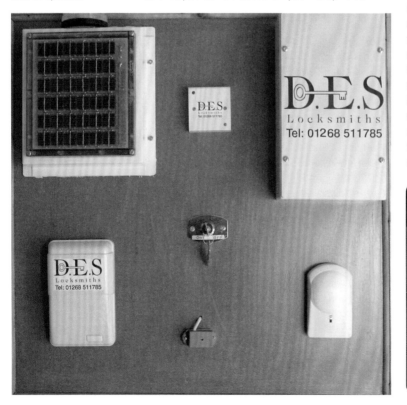

Info

British insurers established the Motor Insurance Repair Research Centre or Thatcham, as it is widely known, in 1969. The centre is independently operated and is a 'not-for-profit' organisation. Thatcham tests vehicle security systems and those for trailers are listed in the 'Q' list for 'non-categorised systems'. Test reports on products can be found on the website www.thatcham.org/security.

Passive electronic systems

These are commonly referred to as tagging systems. They are actually radio frequency identification (RFID) transponders that respond to radio waves sent out by a hand-held tag reader (scanner). They contain:

- all the relevant details about the trailer, including
- the manufacturer and chassis number, and
- the owner's name, address and telephone numbers.

All this information is logged against a unique identity number given to the tag. This information is held on a secure database, accessible to the Police on a 24-hour basis, every day.

Tags take the form of passive (i.e. no power supply) electronic devices that can be supplied in the form of small circular coin-like items, credit card-size tags or in very small glass cylinders the size of large grains of rice.

These are fitted covertly in hidden places on the trailer but there is an overt one from Trovan IDUK Ltd, fitted in a highly visible yellow triangle. This is put in an easily noticeable place on the trailer's drawbar so that the thief is aware that tags are fitted.

If someone removes the marker, evidence is left behind which shows that tags are fitted. The very small glass tags can be 'injected' with adhesive into small, 3mm diameter holes in a wooden floor and are therefore not easily seen at all. The credit card type of tag can be slipped behind the padding in a horse trailer.

The coin-size tags can be glued inside a steel tube or section through an open end. These work when a tag reader (scanner) sends out its radio signal and receives in reply the unique identity number of any tags fitted. Tags cannot be reprogrammed so will always be able to prove the trailer owner's identity. Trovan's 'Stop Theft' trailer kit includes the drawbar transponder as well as one each of the glass and coin types.

There are 3,800 Trovan tag readers in use by police forces in the UK and Eire. Further details can be found by looking at www.rfidsystems.co.uk.

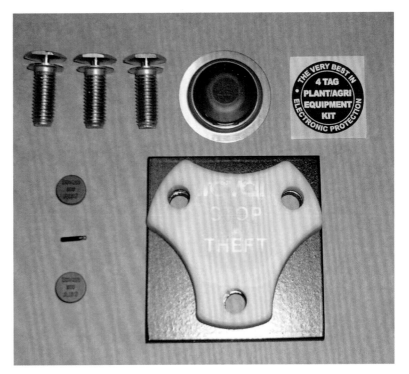

Identity and registration

At the present time, trailers are not required to have an official registration mark from the DVLA. This may come in the future, but it is best to give your trailer its own identity. By fitting tags you are doing this but you can also have the details recorded by companies that work with the Police in order to identify stolen vehicles. Some trailer manufacturers register the trailer's details with the National Plant & Equipment Register, known simply as The Equipment Register (TER) which operates a 24-hour every-day service for the Police and other law enforcement agencies. You can register your trailer with this agency free of cost and it can be contacted through their website www.ter-europe.org.

Another company that provides this service, but with additional features, is Thiefbeaters. This company will visit you and mark your trailer in up to 50 places with a stamped, etched and engraved unique identity number, together with fitting tags and microdots. You are given a registration document telling you what markings and type of marking have been applied to your trailer and their location. They are on call 24 hours every day to help you recover your stolen trailer. This product can enable you to obtain discounts from insurers. Thiefbeaters can also include a tracking system

Trovan Stop Theft kit from Identify UK Ltd.

Thiefbeaters stamped

Etched

Engraved

Thiefbeaters registration document showing locations of markings.

08-10-04

REGISTRATION DOCUMENT

THATCHAM
VEHICLE SECURITY
"Q - Listed"
Recognised by Insurance Companies

Thiefbeaters
Stamping Out Theft

REGISTERED OWNER

Name:	Thiefbeaters
Address:	PO Box 5789
	Towcester
Town:	Northampton
County:	Northants
Post Code:	NN12 8ZJ
Tel.	0870 794 0111

DETAILS OF PROPERTY

Manufacturer:	BATESON TRAILERS
Model:	10' TWIN AXEL
Year:	2005
Colour:	SILVER
Reg No:	NXX XXX
Serial No:	G3XXX2
Vin No:	SBN353XXXXXXX2012
Engine No:	
Est Value:	£ 4,000.00
Other:	HITCH LOCK

Security Star Rating : not applicable

BATESON TRAILERS LIMITED
Marple Stockport England Tel: +44(0) 161-426 0500

UNIQUE IDENTIFICATION NUMBER : TBA1746N

MARK	LOCATION	INSTALLED
STAMPED	AFRAME LHS ON TOP	08-10-2004
STAMPED	AFRAME RHS REAR ONSIDE	08-10-2004
STAMPED	CHASSIS RH FRONT ONSIDE	08-10-2004
ETCHED	LHS FRONT SIDE PANEL BOTTOM LH CORNER	08-10-2004
ETCHED	RHS FRONT SIDE PANEL BOTTOM LH CORNER	08-10-2004
ETCHED	REAR SIDE PANEL TOP RH CORNER	08-10-2004
ETCHED	REAR SIDE PANEL BOTTOM RH CORNER	08-10-2004
ENGRAVED	BELOW SERIAL NUMBER PLATE	08-10-2004
ENGRAVED	HANDBRAKE HANDLE	08-10-2004
ENGRAVED	JOCKEY WHEEL HANDLE AT TOP	08-10-2004

DEVICE	CODE	INSTALLED
Electronic Tag ID 100A F	000662BE9C	08-10-2004
Microdots F	TB30100336	08-10-2004

EMERGENCY PHONE NO

0870 606 4725

Thiefbeaters

PO Box 5789
Towcester
Northants
NN12 8ZJ

Tel: 0870 794 0111
Email: info@thiefbeaters.co.uk
Web: www.thiefbeaters.co.uk

---

when marking your trailer. See their website www.thiefbeaters.co.uk for more details.

Other forms of identity include microdots and smart water. Yellowtag microdots were invented and developed by a team of Master of Business Administration (MBA) graduates from Bath University. Microdots are tiny polycarbonate dots that are laser etched with a freephone number and your own unique identification number. These are registered to you on the Yellowtag international tracking system. In the event of theft or loss the Police can locate the microdots using UV light, whereupon the information is read enabling them to contact you within minutes!

Each pack contains approximately 500 individual microdots suspended in a UV light-traceable adhesive. You simply brush the product over various parts of the trailer to provide up to 500 individual means of identifying it, or its parts if it has been dismantled. Full details can be found on www.yellowtag.com.

Smart water is available for use on trailers in two forms. Smart Water Tracer is an aqueous-based solution with a unique forensic code. Whilst being virtually invisible to the naked eye it glows under UV light and is practically impossible to remove entirely. Smart Water Instant has the additional inclusion of tiny microdot particles which enables the Police to identify the true owner of the property. See www.smartwater.com for details.

You can also put your identity onto a trailer simply by painting it a different colour. If you have a box van trailer it would normally be white but by changing its colour or having it painted 'two tone' means that a thief will think twice before stealing it; its unusual livery would make it stand out from every other trailer. One large UK construction company painted its trailers two tone and this immediately stopped the problem of theft. Similarly, if you use a trailer as part of your business then have it sign written as this immediately identifies it, advertises your services, and means that a thief has to work hard to remove the lettering. This can be surprisingly difficult because you can usually still see where lettering had been placed even when painted over. In effect, this is another deterrent.

On the other hand, if you have a box van trailer do not paint your postcode on the roof; it might alert thieves to the fact that you are not at home! It might be better to paint the last six digits of your chassis number instead.

Yellowtag microdots.

Security product quality

There are no legal requirements for testing security products but the security industry has created its own performance standards. In the UK, the need for performance testing was initiated by the Police and insurance companies. When looking at the packaging of security products you may see various claims as to their performance accreditation with references to agencies like Sold Secure, TÜV and TNO.

Sold Secure is a British company currently run by the Master Locksmiths Association although it was inaugurated by Northumbria and Essex police forces, with the help and backing of the Home Office. Today, Sold Secure tests security devices and awards them Bronze, Silver or Gold status. The tests, referred to by the company as 'attack tests', are very thorough and are carried out using tools that a criminal would use. Bronze products offer a good level of resistance against the opportunist thief and should be used in a normal risk environment. Silver-rated products offer a greater level of resistance against the more determined thief and should be used in a higher risk environment, while Gold-rated products offer the top level of resistance against the dedicated thief and should be used in a high-risk environment. Trailer theft falls into a high-risk environment so you should use, wherever possible, Gold-rated security products. Sold Secure has also developed special test methods to see if electronic security devices can be overcome. To check which products have been tested by Sold Secure and the ratings achieved look at www.soldsecure.com.

TÜV is the major German test house whereas TNO (the Netherlands Organisation for Applied Scientific Research) is a Dutch organisation. Both of these concerns test and certify products and services issuing independent evaluations of product quality.

Trailer insurance companies will most likely specify that the security products you are required to use must conform to one of the above standards.

Recovering your stolen trailer

If you use one of the identification systems above and your trailer is stolen you must contact the company to inform them of the loss

SMARTWATER INSTANT UNDER **NORMAL** LIGHT

SMARTWATER INSTANT UNDER **ULTRAVIOLET** LIGHT

as well as notifying your local police force, in order to be given a crime number. You will need this number if your trailer is insured so that the insurance company knows that you have informed the Police.

The Police will regularly scan any trailers which they believe to be stolen, using tag readers which send out the correct radio signals for reading any RFID tags. They will also use ultraviolet (UV) lamps to see if any microdots or smart water systems were used.

A great help to the Police is to have photographs of your trailer available as these are undoubtedly good evidence of ownership, which may lead to its return. If you have made any modifications these may also help to verify that the retrieved trailer really does belong to you.

TER, mentioned above, regularly attends auctions and checks on any trailers in the sale as auctions are sometimes used to sell stolen property.

What else can you do to help prevent the theft of your trailer?

- Avoid leaving it unattended in full view of a road.
- Store it, if possible, out of sight, as trailers that are on view to people passing your property are the ones most likely to be stolen.
- When storing your trailer make sure that you do use the security devices.
- Do not be tempted to leave them off if you are going to use the trailer again a couple of hours later. That is when it is most likely to disappear.
- Keep it locked to your car while using it, especially if stopping for short periods at a motorway service station.
- Fit your wheel clamp while leaving the outfit parked and unattended.
- If your car has a detachable towball make sure that the ball is locked into the towbar, as thieves will take the trailer with the towball still attached if necessary.

Note the yellow areas showing where Smartwater has been applied.

OWNERS' EXPERIENCES

The following stories show how the needs for a trailer differ greatly according to their owner's hobbies or work activity.

10

They also illustrate the importance of making a list of the specific tasks that you want a trailer to do for you. That way you will buy the most suitable trailer and get the most out of it.

General Purpose type trailer

Derek first started to tow trailers over 40 years ago when he was employed in the building industry. He first used a very second-hand pig trailer but has got through a number of trailers since then. When he moved into his current house he had rather a lot of grass to cut; one and a half acres in fact which produces a large amount of grass cuttings. This quantity needed to be taken away for composting. His trailer at that time was quite old and unsuitable for carrying this material as it had low sides, even after adding wooden extensions, that could not handle such an amount of grass.

This started the search for a trailer that had the design features needed. It had to be unbraked, as the Local Authority's refuse disposal centre allows unbraked trailers in free but charges for receiving refuse carried on braked trailers. The trailer had to have wire-mesh side extensions to handle the volume of cuttings and have flotation tyres that would not sink into wet ground forming ruts that would ruin the appearance of the lawns. It had to have a rear ramp so that the mower could be carried over to a relative's house to cut the lawns there.

A search through the NTTA's website soon found the ideal trailer, a Wessex ATV 220046 model. This has the option of mesh sides and has the 20.5 / 8.00 x 10 4PR large section tyres for use on or off road. The rear ramp design completes the mesh sides making it a most useful trailer.

To save going to and fro all the time when putting the cuttings into the trailer Derek bolted a towball onto the back of the mower and can move the trailer around the lawns placing it in convenient positions.

The trailer has strong mudguards so that Derek can stand on them to compress the load filling the trailer with tree prunings and other garden refuse to take for composting.

The mower can be driven onto the trailer easily and safely when the trailer is hitched to his car and the rear propstands are down. The mower is secured to the built in internal lashing eyes and can then be conveyed to a relative's property to maintain the lawns there.

This trailer has proved to be ideal for its use and shows the value of doing your homework first, making a list of your requirements and then finding the trailer that matches up exactly to your needs.

Horse trailer

Towing a horse trailer became a requirement for Sandy after she was given a Shetland pony named Jasper. Sandy soon realised that Jasper was lonely so she decided to get another Shetland pony to keep him company. Going to horse shows and looking for another pony resulted in Sparkle arriving on permanent loan from an owner who had, due to health problems, had difficulty looking after him.

Whilst she was at a horse competition Sandy was asked to help a competitor in a carriage driving event. She loved this and decided to take up carriage driving thus making it necessary to purchase a horse trailer that could accommodate both ponies and the carriage. It proved to be difficult to find a standard design horse trailer that would easily carry both so Sandy had a look at bespoke horse trailer manufacturers. Pegasus Trailers were able to build one that was tailor-made for her needs.

They collected her carriage and took it to

their factory to make sure that the finished design was just right. It was decided to have the carriage stored at the front with the ponies standing across behind.

The carriage is stored in the front of the trailer.

Sandy's car was not capable of towing this trailer so she had to buy a Land Rover Discovery to tow it. This was quite a change for her to go from driving a family car to a large 4x4 with a big horse trailer behind but she now has the outfit that enables her to take part in carriage driving competitions all over the country.

When she first put forward the idea of using Shetland ponies for these events many people laughed and said that she would not be competitive, as they were thought to be too small. She has certainly proved them wrong by winning a number of events and being placed high up in the British Indoor

Above: The classic British outfit. A Land Rover Discovery and Pegasus horse trailer.

Right: Sandy at speed.

Ready to go!

Driving Championship. The small size of the ponies means that she can take corners much tighter than full size horses and they can go at a surprising speed. They also have what she calls the highest 'wow' factor. This is the response of the audience when she enters the arena with her carriage and Shetlands.

Having a trailer has changed Sandy's life, following her retirement from the teaching profession, so much so that there are now four Shetland ponies in residence. So much for a quiet life!

For Eunice, however, her horse trailer needs differed from Sandy's. She also takes part in pleasure and private carriage driving events but with a large Welsh Cob.

Note the size difference between Eunice's carriage and Sandy's showing that their horse trailer requirements differed considerably.

Eunice wanted a combined horse and living trailer so that she did not have to stay in a Hotel whilst taking part in events. She needed a combination, in fact, of a trailer and a caravan. Pegasus Trailers came up with a design where

Evidently a good day's driving. Her Land Rover Defender and Pegasus outfit can be seen on the left.

the horse is carried at an angle across the front part of the trailer with the living accommodation at the rear. In this design the rear wall is a drop down ramp and with the double bed folded vertically against a sidewall the carriage can be put in place after first removing the carriage's shafts. These are stored in longitudinal tubes attached to the inside of the roof. Removing the carriage on arrival, closing the ramp, dropping down the bed and Eunice is set up to relax before the event.

Box van

For Horn Furniture (UK) Ltd the use of a trailer was for business purposes rather than for the leisure activities shown above. They previously used 7,500kg trucks to deliver and set up their furniture around the UK.

Horn manufacture specialist sewing machine cabinets and computer workstations. The delivery driver unpacks and sets up the

furniture in a customer's home. This, therefore, limits the number of deliveries in a day. A truck had too much unused space so it was decided to try out a VW LT35 van with a GVW of 3,500kg and tow a box van trailer to get the overall load space necessary for a day's deliveries.

Jason Read, of Horn, says that they are making considerable savings in their delivery costs due to:

- Saving on fuel costs. The outfits average 30mpg, which is extremely good and much better than they were achieving with 7,500kg trucks.
- They also save on insurance, as the vans are much cheaper to buy than 7,500kg trucks.
- They save on other running costs, as tyres, batteries, exhausts and servicing are lower than those for trucks.
- They hire the trailers reducing capital costs.

These examples of trailer owners and users show the wide areas in which trailers are utilised. They can operate in every walk of life both leisure and commercial and can enable the owner to take part in hobbies, sport, travel and in business activities. A trailer is a truly flexible vehicle, which deserves greater recognition.

Contact List

4x4 Web
8 Lawrence Mead
Kintbury
Berks RG17 9XT
Tel: 0871 2777160
E-mail: webmaster@4x4web.co.uk
Web: www.4x4web.co.uk
Specialist website for all 4x4 activities, off road schools, clubs, vehicles, parts and action holidays. Useful links to other 4x4 websites.

Acorn Trailers
Unit 1 Carolgate Bridge
108 Carolgate
Retford
Nottinghamshire DN22 6AS
Tel: 01777 862 862
Fax: 01777 862 999
E-mail: mail@acorn-trailers.co.uk
Web: www.acorn-trailers.co.uk
Trailer Manufacturer, Trade and Leisure Mobile Tyre fitting and Repairs, Cars, Vans & Trailers Agents for Metalmec Aluminium Ramps. Trailer & Caravan Tyres. Security products: Wheel & Hitch locks. Trailer Spares.

AL-KO Kober Ltd
South Warwickshire Business Park
Kineton Road
Southam
Warwickshire CV47 0AL
Tel: 01926 818500
Fax: 01926 818562
E-mail: mail@al-ko.co.uk
Web: http://www.al-ko.co.uk
Suppliers of caravan chassis, axles, couplings, stabilisers and spare parts.

Anglian Trailer Centre Ltd
Oak Farm
Cockfield
Bury St Edmunds
Suffolk IP30 0JH
Tel: 01284 828415
Fax: 01284 828912
E-mail: chris@angliantrailers.co.uk
Web: http://www.angliantrailers.co.uk
Suppliers of trailers, parts, servicing and accessories. Trailer Hire.

Bankfarm Trailers Ltd
Robeston Wathen
Narberth
Pembrokeshire SA67 8EN
Tel: 01834 860605
Fax: 01834 861498
E-mail: sales@bankfarm-trailers.co.uk
Web: http://www.bankfarm-trailers.co.uk
Suppliers of trailers, parts, servicing accessories, towbars and towbar fitting. Manufacturer of special trailers. Trailer Hire.

Bankfarm Trailers Ltd has other branches at:

Phase 3
Heol Ffaldau
Brackla Industrial Estate
Bridgend CF31 2AJ
Tel: 01656 649813
Fax: 01656 659742

Spytty Road
Queensway
Newport NP19 4QW
Tel: 01633 290291/279679
Fax: 01633 270400

Millbrook Yard
Landor
Swansea SA1 2JG
Tel: 01792 795834
Fax: 01792 799251

Barlow Trailers
Denizes Farm, Southport Road
Unles Walton, Leyland
Lancashire PR5 3LP
Tel: 01772 600395
Fax: 01772 601389
E-mail: info@barlowtrailers.co.uk
Web: http://www.barlowtrailers.co.uk
Supplier of trailers, servicing, parts, accessories. Trailer Hire.

Bosal UK Ltd
Unit 330, Four Oaks Road
Walton Summit Centre
Preston
Lancs PR5 8AP
Tel: 07768 302429
Fax: 01772 771341
E-mail: peter.redgate@eur.bosal.com
Web: http://www.bosal.com/unitedkingdom
Bosal is a leading supplier of towbars for passenger and light commercial vehicles. Bosal's towbar types include flange ball, swan neck, AK4, AK6 & ecofit detachable, each of which is 94/20/EC type approved. Bosal also offers a complimentary range of vehicle specific wiring kits.

BPW Limited
Legion Way
Meridian Business Park
Leicester LE19 1UZ
Tel: 0116 2816100
Parts Direct Tel: 0116 2816123
Fax: 0116 2816140
E-mail: sales@bpw.co.uk
Web: http://www.bpw.co.uk
Supplier of caravan chassis, axles, Winterhoff stabilisers and spare parts.

Bradley Doublelock Ltd
Victoria Works, Victoria Street
Bingley
W.Yorks BD16 2NH
Tel: 01274 560414
Fax: 01274 551114
E-mail: larry.lambert@bradleydoublelock.co.uk;
glenn.tanner@bradleydoublelock.co.uk
Web: http://www.bradleydoublelock.co.uk
Manufacturer of Axles, Couplings, Jockey Wheels &
related components. Hydraulic disc brake systems.
Vehicle mounted combination and semi-automatic
combination couplings.

Brian James Trailers Ltd
Sopwith Way
Drayton Field Industrial Estate
Daventry
Northants NN11 5PB
Tel: 01327 308833
Fax: 01327 308822
E-mail: send via the website
Web: www.brianjames.co.uk

Brink UK Ltd
Unit 7, Centrovell Ind. Estate
Caldwell Road
Nuneaton
Warwickshire CV11 4NG
Tel: 02476 352353
Fax: 02476 352024
E-mail: donald.thompson@brinkweb.co.uk
Web: http://www.brinkweb.com
Manufacturer and Distributor of Towbars

Bulldog Security Products Ltd
Units 1–4
Stretton Road Ind. Estate
Much Wenlock
Shropshire TF13 6DH
Tel: 01952 728171
Fax: 01952 728117
E-mail: sales@bulldogsecure.com
Web: http://www.bulldogsecure.com
Manufacturer of Stabilisers, Hitchlocks,
Wheelclamps, Security Posts, Ground Anchors and
Chains. Trailer Alarms plus Boat and Jet Ski Security.

Chester Tow-Bar & Trailer Centre
Unit 19, Hartford Way, Sealand Trading Estate
Chester
Cheshire CH1 4NT
Tel: 01244 324034
Fax: 01204 377887
Trailer service and hire. Towbar fitting.

Cruickshank Trailers
Unit 10, Horn Park Quarry Ind Est
Beaminster
Dorset DT8 3TT
Tel: 01308 867 800
Fax: 01308 867 801
E-mail: cruicktrail@aol.com
Web: http://www.cruickshanktrailers.co.uk
Sales & Hire of trailers. Sale of Trailer Parts &
Accessories.

D. E. S. Locksmith
110–112 Furtherwick Road
Canvey Island
Essex
SS8 7AL
Tel: 01268 511785
E-mail: ncrossman5@aol.com
Web: http://www.locallifedesign.co.uk/
clients/deslocksmiths/index2.htm
Suppliers of solar powered alarm systems and
Bulldog Security Products.

Diesel Tuning UK LTD
96m Front Street
Stanley
Co. Durham
DH9 0HU
Tel: 0845 257 2308
Fax: 0845 257 9208
E-mail: sales@dieseltuninguk.com
Web: www.dtuk.biz / dieseltuninguk.com
Supplier of Powerklick tuning units.

Dixon-Bate Ltd
Unit 45, First Avenue
Deeside Ind. Park
Deeside
Flintshire
CH5 2LG
Tel: 01244 288925
Fax: 01244 288462
E-mail: sales@dixonbate.co.uk
Web: http://www.dixonbate.co.uk
Manufacturer of Towing Brackets & Accessories for
4 x 4 & Light Commercial Vehicles, Universal
Couplings,
Adjustable Height Towbars, Shocklink,
Rapide Boat Trailers & West Mersea Marine Trailers.

EZ Rise Trailer Solutions Ltd
Preston House
Long Meadow Lane
Thornton Clevelys
Lancs
FY5 4JT
Tel: 01253 875840
Fax: 01253 875840
E-mail: info@ezrisetrailersolutions.co.uk
Web:
http://www.ezrisetrailersolutions.co.uk
Manufacturer of Trailers & Suspension Units
(pneumatic), Sales of M/C Trailers, Box
Trailers, Boat Trailers, Leisure &
General Purpose Trailers, Repair Work carried out.
Drive-Rite, Air Rite Suspensions and Stabilisers.

Gobur Caravans Ltd
Peacock Way
Melton Constable,
Norfolk
NR24 2BY
Tel: 01263 860031
Fax: 01263 861494
E-mail: info@goburcaravans.co.uk
Web: http://www.goburcaravans.co.uk/
Suppliers of Carousel Folding Caravans.

Graham Edwards Trailers Ltd
Moor Lane
Full Sutton
Stamford Bridge
York
YO4 1HX
Tel: 01759 373062
Fax: 01759 372929
E-mail: sales@edwardstrailers.co.uk
Web: http://www.edwardstrailers.co.uk
Manufacturer & Sales of livestock & general trailers.

Grayston Engineering Ltd
115 Roebuck Road
Chessington
Surrey KT9 1JZ
Telephone: 020 8974 1122
Fax: 020 8974 2288
E-mail: sales@grayston.biz
Web:
http://www.graystonengineering.com
Suppliers of suspension assisters, coil spring kits.

Halfords Plc
Redditch
Worcestershire
B98 0DE
Tel: 0870 870 8810
Fax: 01527 513529
Web: www.halfords.com
Suppliers of Erdé trailers and towing accessories.

Hazlewood Engineering Co Ltd
Bishampton Road
Rous Lench
Nr. Evesham
Worcestershire
WR11 4UN
Tel: 01386 792916
Fax: 01386 793320
Trailer manufacturer, Sales, Hire, Service, Spares.

Hills Numberplates Ltd.
Unit 6, Junction 6 Business Park
Electric Avenue
Witton
Birmingham
B6 7JJ
Tel: 0121 623 8050
Fax: 0121 623 8099
Web: www.hillsnumberplates.com
Suppliers of number plates and number plate production equipment.

Identify UK Limited
Tag House
Prestongate
Hessle
East Yorkshire
HU13 0RD
Tel: 01482 222070
Fax: 01482 327214
E-mail: info@rfidsystems.co.uk
Web: www.rfidsystems.co.uk
Suppliers of Trovan Radio Frequency Identification Tag Systems.

Ifor Williams Trailers
Cynwyd
Corwen
Denbighshire
LL21 0LB
Tel: 01490 412626
Fax: 01490 412770
E-mail: sales@iwt.co.uk
Web: http://www.iwt.co.uk
Manufacturers of Trailers, Containers & Pick-up Canopies.

Knott-Avonride Limited
Europa House
Wharf Road
Burton-on-Trent
Staffordshire
DE14 1PZ
Tel: 01283 531541
Fax: 01283 534840
E-mail: sales@knottuk.com
Web: http://www.knottuk.com
Manufacturer and Importer of Brakes (spreadlever, cam, hydro, disc, oil immersed etc), Cables, Overrun Couplings, Jockey Wheels and ancilliary equipment for the Trailer, Caravan, Fork Lift Truck and Transmission Industries. Overrun Couplings, cast, pressed steel, square tube, adj. height; Jockey Wheels (leisure and commercial).

Land Rover Administration
Freepost TK494
Twickenham TW2 5UN
For test drive or brochure enquires
Telephone: 0800 110 110.
Web: www.landrover.com
Manufacturers of 4x4 vehicles.

Marco Trailers
83 Railway Road
Newhaven
East Sussex
BN9 0AP
Tel: 01273 513718
Fax: 01273 512132
E-mail: info@marcotrailers.co.uk
Web: http://www.marcotrailers.co.uk
Design and manufacture of quality purpose-built exhibition, display, promotion and merchandising trailers (including field/on-site operational units), both trailed and motorised.

Peak Trailers Ltd
Waterloo Industrial Estate, Waterloo Road
Bidford-on-Avon
Warwickshire
B50 4JH
Tel: 01789 778041
Fax: 01789 490331
E-mail: sales@peaktrailers.com
Web: http://www.peaktrailers.com
Light Trailer Axles, Suspension Units, Couplings.

Pegasus Trailers
(See Wessex Trailers Ltd.)

Peter Bowman Towing Centre
1–37 Mason Street
Bury
Lancs BL9 0RH
Tel: 0161 797 3000
Fax: 0161 761 1579
E-mail: peter@towing.co.uk
Web: http://www.towing.co.uk/
Trailers Sales, Service, Hire. Tow-Bar fitting.

Rhino Developments
5 Kings Court, Willie Snaith Rd, Newmarket
Suffolk CB8 7SG
Tel: 01638 675760
Fax: 01638 675769
E-mail: info@rhinodevelopments.co.uk
Web: http://www.rhinodevelopments.co.uk/
Manufacturers and Suppliers of Ground Anchors, Chains and Locks.

Right Connections (UK) Ltd
5 Rose Crescent
Wellington, Telford
Shropshire TF1 1HT
Tel: 01952 249 333
E-mail: enquiries@rightconnections.co.uk
Web: http://www.rightconnections.co.uk
Suppliers of vehicle specific towbar wiring harnesses, including ECU versions and WeSt Multicon connectors.

R. M. Trailers Ltd
Prospect Road, New Farm Industrial Estate
New Alresford
Hants SO24 9QF
Tel: 01962 732560
Fax: 01962 734027
E-mail: rmtrailers@aol.com
Web: www.rmtrailers.co.uk

SAS Products Ltd
Chestnut House, Chesley Hill
Wick
Bristol BS30 5NE
Tel: 0117 937 4747 or 4737
Fax: 0117 937 4642
Email: Shop@SASproducts.com
Web: http://www.sasproducts.co.uk/
Suppliers of Wheel Clamps, Hitchlocks, Alarm systems, Tracking Systems and Straightliner Stabiliser.

SEB International Ltd
Unity Road,
Lowmoor Business Park,
Kirkby In Ashfield,
Nottinghamshire NG17 7LE
United Kingdom
Tel: 01623 754490
Fax: 01623 753477
E-mail: andrew@sebinternational.com
Web: http://www.sebinternational.co.uk
Plant trailers, generator set trailers, cable drum trailers and special projects

Siemens VDO Trading Limited
36 Gravelly Industrial Park
Birmingham B24 8TA
Tel: 0121 326 1234
Fax: 0121 326 1298
E-mail: uk@siemensvdo.com
Web: www.vdo.com
Suppliers of Tachographs.

SmartWater Technology Limited
PO Box 136
Telford
Shropshire TF3 3WY
Telephone: 0870 242 8899
Fax: 0870 242 4561
E-mail: enquiry@smartwater.com
Web: http://www.smartwater.com
Suppliers of the Smartwater Forensic Coding System.

Sold Secure
5c Great Central Way
Woodford Halse
Daventry
Northants
NN11 3PZ
Tel: 01327 264687
Fax: 01327 264686
E-mail: admin@soldsecure.com
Web: www.soldsecure.com
Test House for Security Products.

Mule Security Products
PO Box 2145
Westhoughton
Bolton
BL6 9AX
Tel: 0808 178 1860
Web: www.supamule.com
Supplier of security products.

Tanfield Limited
Blatchford Road
Horsham
West Sussex
RH13 5QR
Tel: 01403 269100
Fax: 01403 251199
E-mail: keith@tanfieldtowing.co.uk
Web: http://www.tanfieldtowing.co.uk
Sales/Retailer of Towing Brackets, Trailers and related accessories.

TER
The National Plant & Equipment Register,
Bath & West Buildings,
Lower Bristol Road,
Bath
BA2 3EG
United Kingdom
Tel: 01225 464599
Fax: 01225 317698
E-mail: info@ter-europe.org
Web: www.ter-europe.org
Provides an identity for a trailer through free registration. Police have full access to the register.

Tetton Trailers
Bridge Farm
Tetton Lane
Moston
Middlewich
Cheshire
CW10 0HH
Tel: 01270 526171
Fax: 01270 526118
E-mail: sales@tettontrailers.co.uk
Web: http://tettontrailers.co.uk
Sales / Hire of 3 Way Tippers, Horse, Livestock, M/Cycle, Car Transporters, Cargoliners, Platform, Camping, ATV, Lawnmower & Boat trailers. Roof Systems Hire/Sales.

TH Motors
Redcap Garage
Blackburn Road
Blackburn
Lancs.
BB1 3LS
Tel: 01254 675522
Fax: 01254 681953
E-mail: info@trailersandtowbars.co.uk
Web: http://www.trailersandtowbars.co.uk
Trailer sales, Hire, Servicing, Repairs. Tow-bar fitting.

The Camping and Caravanning Club
Greenfields House
Westwood Way
Coventry
West Midlands
CV4 8JH
Tel: 02476 47 5282
Fax: 02476 47 5413
E-mail: send via the website
Web: www.campingandcaravanningclub.co.uk
Provider of Camping and Caravanning Information and Services.

The Caravan Club
East Grinstead House
East Grinstead
West Sussex
RH19 1UA
Tel: 01342 336897
Fax: 01342 410258
E-mail: enquiries@caravanclub.co.uk
Web: http://www.caravanclub.co.uk
A members club for users of Caravans, Trailer Tents and Motor Caravans.

The Pennine Group
Chester Street
Accrington
Lancashire
BB5 0SD
Tel: 01254 385991
Fax: 01254 386111
E-mail: sales@pennine-leisure.co.uk
Web: www.thepenninegroup.co.uk
Manufacturer of Pennine Folding Campers and Conway Trailer Tents.

Thiefbeaters Ltd
PO Box 5789,
Towcester,
Northants NN12 8ZJ.
Tel: 0870 444 0789
Fax: 0870 444 9707
Email: info@thiefbeaters.co.uk
Web: www.thiefbeaters.co.uk
Providers of the Thiefbeaters permanent identification system.

Towability Trailers (Time Leisure Ltd)
Nene Court
The Embankment
Wellingborough
Northamptonshire NN8 1LD
Tel: 01933 229025
Fax: 01933 227049
E-mail: sales@towability.com
Web: http://www.towability.com
Manufacture, Sales Servicing & Repair of Catering Trailers, Caravans, Hospitality Trailers.

Towbars & Trailers
Davian Works
Storforth Lane
Chesterfield
Derbyshire S40 2TU
Tel: 01246 202543/236378
Fax: 01246 551119
E-mail: anthony.maris@which.net
Web: http://www.towitall.co.uk
Towbar fitting including one-off towbars for motorhomes etc. Trailer manufacturer plus hire, sales, spares, repairs, servicing and alterations. Caravan servicing, resealing and accessories. Extensive brake spare parts. Towbar wiring kits and components. Boat bits. Mail order.

Towcraft Ltd
20–22 Birmingham Road
Rowley Regis
West Midlands B65 9BL
Tel: 0121 561 3351
Fax: 0121 559 1398
E-mail: mail@towcraft.co.uk
Web: http://www.towcraft.co.uk
Towbar Sales, Fitting & Distributors. Trailer Sales, Servicing, Accessories & Spares. Roof Systems & Boxes. Cycle Carriers, Spring Assisters and Stabilisers.

Towing Solutions Ltd
The Old Dyehouse
London Road Terrace
Macclesfield
Cheshire
SK11 7RN
Tel: 01625 433251
Fax: 08712 425404
E-mail: info@towing-solutions.co.uk
Web: http://www.towing-solutions.co.uk
Trailer Driving School – specialist B+E licence training and Health at Work trailer driver tuition. Towing law presentation. We provide courses for commercial, utilities and private groups and individuals. Our aim is to help you be a safe and successful trailer driver.

TrailerTek
Warren Farm, Micheldever Station
Winchester
Hampshire SO21 3AS
Tel: 01962 774988
Fax: 01962 795093
E-mail: karl@trailertek.com
Web: http://www.trailertek.com
Trailer Sales, Service and Repairs. Trailer Hire: Large fleet, low rates. Trailer Parts for all makes: On-line catalogue Towbar Fitting.

Treales Trailers
Foundry Yard, Treales
Preston
Lancashire PR4 3SD
Tel & Fax: 01772 673184
Email: enquiries@treales-trailers.c.uk
Web: www.trealestrailers/co.uk
Solomatic Sovereign 'A' Frame and Stowboy towing dolly. Budget line box and motorcycle trailers. Brenderup trailers. Trailer parts and accessories. Bulldog Security Products.

University of Worcester
Henwick Grove
WR2 6AJ
Tel: 01905 855000
E-mail: info@marrc.co.uk
Web: www.marrc.co.uk
Motion Analysis Research and Rehabilitation Centre at the University of Worcester.

Watsonian-Squire Ltd
Northwick Business Centre
Blockley, Glos. GL56 9RF
Tel: 01386 700907
Fax: 01386 700738
E-mail: peter@watsonian-squire.com
Web: www.watsonian-squire.com
Manufacturers of Motorcycle Trailers and Sidecars.

Wessex Trailers Ltd
Waddock Cross
Dorchester
Dorset
DT2 8QY
Tel: 01929 462534
Fax: 01929 405034
E-mail: sales@wessex-trailers.co.uk
Web: http://www.wessex-trailers.co.uk
Trailer manufacturers. Extensive range includes unbraked & braked goods & platform trailers, plant, digger & tippers, van, livestock & horseboxes. Tilt decks and tilting car transporters. Pegasus Horse Trailers.

In addition Wessex has another branch:

Wessex Trailers (Birmingham)
192 Bridge Street West
Newtown
Aston
Birmingham
B19 2YT
Tel: 0121 359 6387 / 0121 359 6343
E:mail sales@birminghamtrailers.co.uk

Witter Towbars
Drome Road
Deeside Industrial Park
Deeside
Flintshire
CH5 2NY
Tel: 01244 284500
Fax: 01244 284577
E-mail: sales@witter-towbars.co.uk
Web: http://www.witter-towbars.co.uk
Design & Manufacture of Towbars, Adjustable Height Couplings, Towbar Mounted Steps and Bumper Protection System.

Useful Contacts

For the interpretation of the laws relating to towing including Construction and Use, Vehicle Lighting, Tachographs and Towbars contact:
Department for Transport
Great Minster House, 76 Marsham Street, London SW1P 4DR
Telephone 020 7944 8300
www.dft.gov.uk

For interpretation of the laws relating to Driving Licences contact:
Driver and Vehicle Licensing Agency
Swansea SA6 7JL
Telephone 0870 240 0009
www.dvla.gov.uk

For information on and booking of B+E Towing Tests contact:
Driving Standards Agency
Stanley House, 56 Talbot Street, Nottingham NG1 5GU
Telephone 0115 901 2500
www.dsa.gov.uk

For information on type approvals contact:
Vehicle Certification Agency
No 1 The Eastgate Office Centre, Eastgate Road, Bristol BS5 6XX
Telephone 0117 951 5151
www.vca.gov.uk

For general information on towing and locating trailer and towbar manufacturers, towbar fitters and trailer centres contact:
National Trailer and Towing Association
1 Alveston Place, Leamington Spa, Warwickshire CV32 4SN
Telephone 01926 335445
www.ntta.co.uk

To find European Directives and Regulations go to EUR-Lex at
http://europa.eu.int/eur-lex/lex/RECH_legislation.do

To find United Nations Economic Commission for Europe Transport Regulations go to:
http://www.unece.org/trans/main/wp29/wp29regs.html

To find British Regulations go to The Office of Public Sector Information website at
http://www.opsi.gov.uk/legislation/about_legislation.htm

For information on tyres go to the European Tyre and Rim Technical Organisation at
http://www.etrto.org/home.html

Directives, Laws and Standards

A list of the European Directives, British laws and British and European Standards relating to towing:

European Directives:
71/320/EC Trailer Braking System
91/439/EC Driving Licences 2nd Directive
94/20/EC Type Approval of Trailer Couplings and Towbars
95/3820/EC Drivers' Hours
95/48/EC European Whole Vehicle Type Approval – Weights and Measurements
98/12/EC Asbestos Free Brake friction materials
98/2411/EC European Flag on Number Plates

British Laws:
Road Traffic Regulations Act 1984 (ss 81-91and schedule 6) Speed Limits
The Road Traffic Act 1988 (c.52)
The Road Vehicles (Construction & Use) Regulations 1986 (SI 1986 No. 1078)
The Road Vehicles (Display of Registration Marks) 2001 (SI 2001 No. 561)
The Road Vehicles Lighting Regulations 1989 (SI 1989 No. 1796)
The Road Vehicles (Authorisation of Special Types) (General) Order 2003 (SI 2003 No. 1998)
Recovery of broken down vehicles
Transport Act 1968 Part VI Drivers' Hours
Welfare of Animals (Transport Order) 1997 (SI 1997 No. 1480)

British and European Standards:
BS 4626 : 1970 Specification for touring trailer caravans
BS 6765-4 : 1987 Specification for caravan undergear
BS 7691 : 2004 Specification for Nose Weight Gauge
BS AU 113c : 1978 Trailer Couplings 50mm ball
BS AU 114b : 1979 Strength requirement for Couplings and towballs
BS AU 145d : 1998 Specification for Vehicle number plates
BS AU 149a : 1980 Electrical connection type 12N
BS AU 175-1b : 1983 VIN Specification and content
BS AU 175-2b : 1983 VIN World Manufacturer Codes (WMI)
BS AU 175-3b : 1983 VIN Location and attachment
BS AU 175-4a : 1997 Vehicle Identification Numbers (VIN)
BS AU 177a : 1980 Electrical connection type 12S
BS AU 194 : 1984 Performance for electrical connections between car and trailer
BS AU 210-1 : 1987 Drawbars for caravans and light trailers
BS AU 210-2 : 1994 Drawbars and chassis for caravans and trailers in Aluminium
BS AU 24a : 1989 Trailer Couplings Eye and Jaw / Pin types up to 5000kg
BS AU 267 : 1998 Code of Practice for Breakaway Cables and Secondary Couplings
BS AU 50-3.7 : 1985 Tyre and Wheels Code of Practice
BS EN 1648-1 : 2004 Low voltage installations in Caravans
BS EN ISO 11446 : 2004 Electrical connection 13 pin type

Acknowledgements

The author and publishers thank the many people in the industry for their support in the preparation of this manual particularly:

John Wickersham for reading every word, giving invaluable help in making the words flow more easily and providing diagrams and photographs.

Tony Maris of Towbars & Trailers for his help on towbar relay wiring diagrams and modifications to the wiring for better performance.

Nick Harding of The Camping and Caravanning Club for his help at the beginning of this project.

Knott – Avonride Ltd. for their help on trailer braking systems.

The National Trailer and Towing Association and the following members:

Acorn Trailers	www.acorn-trailers.co.uk
AL-KO Kober Ltd.	www.al-ko.co.uk
Anglian Trailer Centre Ltd.	www.angliantrailers.co.uk
Bankfarm Trailers Ltd.	www.bankfarm-trailers.co.uk
Barlow Trailers	www.barlowtrailers.co.uk
Bosal UK Ltd.	www.bosal.com/unitedkingdom
Bradley Doublelock Ltd.	www.bradleydoublelock.co.uk
Brink UK Ltd.	www.brinkweb.com
Bulldog Security Products Ltd.	www.bulldogsecure.com
Chester Tow-bar & Trailer Centre	
Cruickshank Trailers	www.cruickshanktrailers.co.uk
Dixon-Bate Ltd. (and Rapide Boat trailers)	www.dixonbate.co.uk
EZ Rise Trailer Solutions Ltd.	www.ezrisetrailersolutions.co.uk
Graham Edwards Trailers Ltd.	www.edwardstrailers.co.uk
Hazlewood Engineering Co. Ltd.	
Ifor Williams Trailers	www.iwt.co.uk
Knott-Avonride Ltd.	www.knottuk.com
Marco Trailers	www.marcotrailers.co.uk
Peak Trailers Ltd.	www.peaktrailers.com
Pegasus Trailers	www.pegasus-trailers.co.uk
Right Connections (UK) Ltd.	www.rightconnections.co.uk
Tanfield Ltd.	www.tanfieldtowing.co.uk
Tetton Trailers	www.tettontrailers.co.uk
The Camping and Caravanning Club	www.campingandcaravanningclub.co.uk
The Caravan Club	www.caravanclub.co.uk
Time Leisure Ltd. (Towability Trailers)	www.towability.com
Towbars and Trailers	www.towitall.co.uk
Towcraft Ltd.	www.towcraft.co.uk
Towing Solutions Ltd.	www.towing-solutions.co.uk
TrailerTek	www.trailertek.com
Wessex Trailers Ltd.	www.wessex-trailers.co.uk
Witter Towbars	www.witter-towbars.co.uk

In addition to the author the following companies provided photographs:

4x4 Web	www.4x4web.co.uk
BPW	www.bpw.co.uk
Diesel Tuning UK Ltd.	www.dtuk.biz
Gobur Caravans Ltd.	www.goburcaravans.co.uk
Grayston Engineering Ltd.	www.graystonengineering.com
Hills Numberplates Ltd.	www.hillsnumberplates.com
Mule Security Products	www.supamule.com
Rhino Developments	www.rhinodevelopments.co.uk
R. M. Trailers Ltd.	www.rmtrailers.co.uk
SAS Products Ltd.	www.sasproducts.co.uk
SEB International Ltd.	www.sebinternational.com
Smartwater Technology Ltd.	www.smartwater.com
The Pennine Group (Conway)	www.thepenninegroup.co.uk
Thiefbeaters Ltd.	www.thiefbeaters.co.uk
Treales Trailers	www.trealestrailers/co.uk
University of Worcester	www.worcester.ac.uk
Watsonian – Squire Ltd.	www.watsonian-squire.com
Yellowtag Limited	www.yellowtag.com

Special thanks to:

Halfords
for supplying the Erde trailer kit.
www.halfords.com

Ifor Williams Trailers
for supplying additional photos.
www.iwt.co.uk

Land Rover UK
for supplying the excellent new Discovery HSE.
www.landrover.com

Witter Towbars
for supplying and fitting towbars.
www.witter-towbars.co.uk

Finally very special thanks to Louise McIntyre, Project Manager, Books Division of Haynes Publishing and her team who have encouraged me along the way and converted my work into this quality book.

Index